D0340045

Jane Austen
Structure and Social Vision

Edited by David Monaghan

JANE AUSTEN IN A SOCIAL CONTEXT

823
A933J
M734j

→ JANE AUSTEN
STRUCTURE AND
SOCIAL VISION

David Monaghan

BARNES & NOBLE
BOOKS
10 East 53d St., New York 10022
(a division of Harper & Row Publishers, Inc.)

28.50

71450

© David Monaghan 1980

All rights reserved. No part of this publication may be reproduced or transmitted, in any form or by any means, without permission

First published 1980 by
THE MACMILLAN PRESS LTD
London and Basingstoke

First published in the U.S.A. 1980 by
HARPER & ROW PUBLISHERS INC.
BARNES & NOBLE IMPORT DIVISION

British Library Cataloging in Publication Data

Monaghan, David
  Jane Austen, structure and social vision
  1. Austen, Jane – Criticism and interpretation
  I. Title
  823'.7   PR4037

MACMILLAN ISBN 0–333–27110–6

BARNES & NOBLE ISBN 0–06–494914–1
LCN 79–53866

Printed in Hong Kong

To Gail

Contents

Acknowledgements

The research and writing which have resulted in this book were greatly assisted by the Canada Council (now known as the Social Sciences and Humanities Research Council of Canada) and by Mount Saint Vincent University. I am indebted to the former for research grants, given in 1974 and 1976, and for a Leave Fellowship in 1977/78; and to the latter for a sabbatical leave grant in 1977/78.

Chapter 3, *Pride and Prejudice* and Chapter 6, *Persuasion*, first appeared, in somewhat different form, as 'The Novel and its Age: a Study of Theme and Structure in *Pride and Prejudice*', *Humanities Association Review*, 28 (1977) 151–66, and as 'The Decline of the Gentry: a Study of Jane Austen's Attitude to Formality in *Persuasion*', *Studies in the Novel*, 7 (1975) 73–87. I am grateful to the editors of the *Humanities Association Review* and *Studies in the Novel* for permission to reprint this material.

Introduction: The Novels and Their World

Jane Austen's novels are seamless. The critic can enter at any point and still trace the pattern. So Stuart Tave contends, and demonstrates by picking up single words like 'lively' and using them to take the reader to the heart of Jane Austen's achievement.[1] It is doubtful, though, if many critics review all the possibilities before selecting an approach. Rather, they are directed by a combination of personal interest or prejudice and an instinctive sense of what is really important in her novels. Certainly, nothing more than this was at work in my original decision that a study of the formal social occasion would illuminate Jane Austen's art. In retrospect, though, I can claim that my instincts were at least in tune with my own views on what is important in literature; the formal social occasion turns out to be an appropriate point of entry into Jane Austen's novels because it demonstrates very precisely how she achieves that integration of social vision and artistic form which characterises all great fiction.

I have just suggested that a study of social rituals, by which I mean events like balls, dinners, evening-parties and visits, will help us understand how Jane Austen viewed her society. These are not the kind of activities that we would normally expect to be very revealing of social attitudes, and the link between the two clearly needs some explanation. For this we must look first at the social context out of which her novels grew. English society in the late eighteenth century was largely made up of a series of rural communities governed in paternalistic fashion from the great house by a member of the gentry or the aristocracy who owed his authority and prestige to the ownership of land.[2] Each community included a cross-section of the ranks and was, by and large, independent of all others. Links were created, however, by meetings between the landowners during county activities, such as fox-hunting, and by the congregation of the greatest of them in London for the season.[3]

Starting, then, with the vertical relationships that stretched from highest to lowest in the village, and proceeding to the horizontal connections between members of the small ruling élite, a network of face-to-face contacts was created which embraced all of society. The existence of this network was fundamental to the ruling class's conception of what the state should be; as David Spring puts it: 'Social relations were for [the landowner] personal relations.'[4] Therefore, anything that threatened it, such as the creation of large, centralised institutions, or the growth of cities, was viewed with distaste. The Government at Westminster was expected to restrict itself to maintaining law and order, conducting foreign affairs and waging wars; London was loathed as a place of anonymity which harboured all kinds of vice and sedition.[5]

To understand the broader social vision out of which this intense concern with personal relationships springs we must turn briefly to Edmund Burke, the great philosopher of the landed interest. According to Burke, the state is not a crude contrivance of man, but a finely-tuned creation of God, a complex organism no part of which is redundant or alienated from any other part. Indeed, each component, whether it be the primary one of the individual, or the basic social groupings of the family and the small community, is a microcosm of the whole: 'To be attached to the subdivision, to love the little platoon we belong to in society, is the first principle (the germ as it were) of publick affections. It is the first link in the series by which we proceed towards a love to our country and to mankind.'[6] Consequently, if any part fails, the state suffers; if enough parts fail, the state fails. Conversely, if the individual, the family and the community flourish, the nation prospers. The well-being of the state is therefore directly related to the quality of the relationships that the individual is able to establish with his immediate family and his community.

Granted the tremendous significance which it attached to personal relationships, it is inevitable that this society should have placed particular emphasis on the individual's obligations to recognise the needs of others and to strive to meet these needs. And, indeed, the right of the landed gentleman to rule resided finally in the belief that he was better situated than members of other groups to live up to such obligations. The banker and merchant might have had incomes as large as the landowner's, but they had to work for theirs. The landowner's wealth, on the other hand, was unearned, and this meant that he had leisure. In the eighteenth century leisure was not equated with idleness. On the contrary it 'was the ideal at which the whole society aimed'[7] because, without it, it was considered unlikely that the individual could develop the level of disinterestedness necessary if he were to place the general welfare above his own. The man who had to earn his living, it was believed, tended either to be completely caught up in the business of survival, or, even worse, to regard the making of money as an end in itself. The landed gentleman's situation in life further discouraged self-interestedness in that the estate which he controlled was not regarded as his to do with as he liked, but as the property of future generations to whom he must pass it on whole:

> But one of the first and most leading principles on which the commonwealth and laws are consecrated, is lest the temporary possessors and life-renters in it, unmindful of what they have received from their ancestors, or what is due to their posterity, should act as if they were the entire masters.[8]

There were numerous practical ways in which the landowner could fulfil his obligations to that wide circle of acquaintances he called his 'friends'. He might have a political office or a living to give to a member of another landed family, or he might be able to provide a poor tenant with access to a charity. Even paupers would not have escaped his attention, and any lucky enough to be attached to his parish were guaranteed protection.[9] However, more important than any act of patronage were the ritual means by which he could express an awareness of the needs of others. As Burke puts it:

> Manners are of more importance than laws. Upon them, in a great measure, the laws depend. The law touches us but here and there, and now and then. Manners are what vex and soothe, corrupt or purify, exalt or debase, barbarize or refine us . . . They give their whole form and colour to our lives. According to their quality, they aid morals, they supply them, or they totally destroy them.[10]

When Burke suggests that manners do more than touch us 'here and there, and now and then', he is pointing to their greatest strength. Not even the most influential of landowners could actively demonstrate his concern for others as often and in as many different situations as was possible through polite behaviour. What was true for the landowner was, of course, all the more true for men of lower rank, who had little patronage to dispense, and for women, regardless of their social position, because they had few chances to be of direct use to others beyond the confines of the home.[11] Only through the medium of good manners could these people hope to live up to the ideals established by the landed gentleman. The health of society, then, was felt to depend above all on an infinite number of tiny ritual gestures of concern, each one of which contributed to harmonious relationships between individuals and between ranks, and within families and communities.

When he speaks of manners, Burke is not of course referring just to delicate questions of etiquette, but rather to that whole complex of gestures, both of speech and body, by which one individual acknowledges his awareness of the unique existence of another. Nevertheless, it is in his more formal social contacts that the quality of a person's polite performance is most severely tested. Therefore, in the eighteenth century 'the ceremonies of life' (*Mansfield Park*, 93)[12] were characterised by particularly strict codes of behaviour. Philip J. S. Richardson's account of the balls held at Bath under the auspices of Nash gives us a good sense of this concern with formality:

Each ball was to open with a minuet danced by two persons of the highest distinction present. The lady then retired to her seat and Mr Nash brought the gentleman a new partner. This ceremony was to be observed by every succeeding couple, every gentleman being obliged to dance with two ladies until the minuets, which generally lasted two hours, were over. At eight the country dances were to begin, ladies of quality, according to their rank, standing up first. At nine came a short interval for rest and tea. Country dances were then resumed until the clock struck eleven when, even if in the middle of a dance, the ball terminated.[13]

The English dinner party, as de la Rochefoucauld points out, was characterised by a similar emphasis on ceremony:

At four o'clock precisely . . . you must present yourself in the drawing room with a great deal more ceremony than we are accustomed to in France. This sudden change of social manners is quite astonishing and I was deeply struck by it. In the morning you come down in riding-boots and a shabby coat, you sit where you like, you behave as if you were by yourself, no one takes any notice of you, and it is all extremely comfortable. But in the evening, unless you have just arrived, you must be well washed and well groomed. The standard of politeness is uncomfortably high—strangers go first into the dining room and sit near the hostess and are served in seniority in accordance with a rigid etiquette.[14]

If we bear in mind, then, the important part played in eighteenth-century England by the small community, the great house, the landed gentleman, the network of personal contacts, the ideal of concern for others, the system of manners, and the formal social occasion, Jane Austen's novels are revealed as being much more in touch with the main currents of her age than has sometimes been supposed. It is unnecessary to seek out fleeting references to the Napoleonic Wars, the Slave Trade, agricultural change or other 'major' issues of the time, to justify the claim that Jane Austen is a social novelist.[15] Rather, her main subject—polite social relationships between members of the landed classes within the context of the village and the great house—is one that, far from being escapist, takes us immediately to what her society thought of as being its very heart.

The social thrust of Jane Austen's novels is made clear by the type of communities in which she chooses to locate them and by the extremely selective way in which these communities are populated.[16] In a letter to her niece, Anna, giving advice on how to write a novel, Jane Austen states unequivocally that '3 or 4 Families in a Country Village is the very thing to work on'.[17] With the exception of *Emma*, in which the action only once strays beyond the confines of Highbury, she does not in fact stick rigidly to this one type of setting. Cities, most notably London and Bath, but also Portsmouth in *Mansfield Park*, play an important part in the action of all her other novels. Nevertheless, Jane Austen is faithful to the spirit of the dictum. Her major characters may move away from the village or its neighbouring great house from time to time, but it is within these settings that their values are shaped and (apart from Anne Elliot in *Persuasion*) their future lies. Thus the centres of Jane Austen's fictional world are its Bartons, Longbourns, Pemberleys, and Mansfield Parks, not its Londons and Baths. This is essentially true even of *Northanger Abbey*, because, although over half the novel is set in Bath, it plays only a transitional role in Catherine Morland's life, as she moves from one rural community at Fullerton to another at Woodston.

In selecting the '3 or 4 Families' around which her representations of village life were to be constructed, Jane Austen did not attempt to present a demographically accurate cross-section, but rather to give emphasis to those groups which her contemporaries regarded as most important. Consequently, her heroes and heroines almost all come from the ranks of the landowners, particularly the gentry, the class to which Jane Austen herself belonged, because these provided society with its moral leadership.[18] Catherine Morland is the daughter of a clergyman who has 'a considerable independence, besides two good livings' (13); the Dashwood sisters, although relatively impoverished themselves, belong to an old family that owns Norland, an estate worth £4000 a year; Elizabeth Bennet's father possesses an estate worth £2000 a year; Fanny Price is properly the adopted daughter of Sir Thomas Bertram, baronet owner of Mansfield Park and a member of parliament; Emma Woodhouse is a member of an extremely wealthy and long-established family, and has a personal fortune of £30,000; and Anne Elliot's father is the baronet owner of Kellynch Hall. Similarly, Henry Tilney is a clergyman and the younger son of General Tilney, the owner of Northanger Abbey; Edward Ferrars is a clergyman, and heir to £10,000; Colonel Brandon possesses the Barton Park estate, worth £2000 a year; Darcy is the owner of Pemberley, worth £10,000 a year, and keeps a house in London; Edmund Bertram is the younger son of Sir Thomas; and Mr Knightley is a considerable landed gentleman.

The middle classes were not granted any independent moral role, but were expected simply to follow the example set by the landowners. For this reason, Jane Austen gives them rather less attention. However, they were important to her because she realised that they had developed an alternative bourgeois ethic that posed a serious threat to the moral authority of the landed classes. Therefore, characters who either belong to the middle class or who have clear middle-class origins are to be found throughout her novels. Among the most important are John and Isabella Thorpe, the children of a widow from Putney; Lucy and Anne Steele, the nieces of a schoolteacher; Mrs Bennet, whose father was an attorney, and her brother, Mr Gardiner, who is in trade; Mrs Elton, the daughter of a merchant; Mr and Mrs Cole, who have retired after a career in trade; Lieutenant Price, a half-pay officer with no inherited income; and William Walter Elliot, who denied his genteel origins by marrying a butcher's granddaughter. The lower orders in the eighteenth century were considered too ignorant to have any conception of the general welfare. Thus, servants, shopkeepers, ostlers, gypsies and paupers appear only on the fringes of Jane Austen's novels, and play little part in the main action.

Having carefully established the social positions of her characters, Jane Austen is able to use them to demonstrate her thesis that the fate of society depends on the ability of the landed classes to live up to their ideal of concern for others, and on the willingness of the other groups to accept this ideal. To argue this is clearly not unusual for a person of Jane Austen's time and social background. However, what makes her far more than a mere apologist for the ruling class is that, from the beginning of her career, she was very alert to the ways in which the *status quo* was being threatened. In Jane Austen's novels, selfishness impinges on selflessness from a number of directions. Members of the aristocracy, like Lady Catherine de Bourgh and Sir Walter Elliot, too often forget that their high social status brings with it an obligation to attend to the needs of others, and instead value rank as a source of personal glory. People of middle-class origins, such as Isabella Thorpe, Lucy Steele or Mrs Elton, tend to make the acquisition of wealth and status ends in themselves. The gentry is, on the whole, much more clear-sighted about its social obligations. However, even within this group, there are deviants. Some, like General Tilney, who lists the Marquis of Longtown and the Lady Frasers amongst his friends, ape the aristocratic vice of vanity. Others, like John Dashwood, whose wife's background is urban bourgeois, become infected with materialism.

In her early novels, Jane Austen seems to have reasonable confidence that the existing order of things can be maintained despite these discordant elements. In *Northanger Abbey*, *Sense and Sensibility* and *Pride and Prejudice*, snobs like General Tilney, Robert Ferrars and Lady Catherine de Bourgh, and materialists like Isabella and John Thorpe, Wickham and Charlotte Lucas never exercise more than a temporary influence over the heroines, Catherine Morland, Elinor and Marianne Dashwood and Elizabeth Bennet, each of whom is thus able either to acquire or retain a mature sense of consideration for others. And, since all four eventually marry equally worthy men, who are either the spiritual or social leaders of their society—Henry Tilney and Edward Ferrars are clergymen; Colonel Brandon and Darcy landowners—it is clearly with them rather than the forces of corruption that social supremacy rests.

With *Pride and Prejudice*, Jane Austen's faith in the 'old society' reaches its peak. Whereas only the gentry works towards social harmony in *Northanger Abbey* and *Sense and Sensibility*, in *Pride and Prejudice*, Darcy, an aristocrat, and the Gardiners, tradespeople, are employed to show how all the ranks can contribute to the ideal of concern for others. Following this affirmation, however, Jane Austen depicts a much less stable society in *Mansfield Park*. The gentry now appears morally weakened, and the threats posed by an effete aristocracy and a materialistic urban class are very real. Intruders like Yates, the idle nobleman, and the Crawfords from London fill the void created by Sir Thomas Bertram's failings as an authority figure; and the Bertram children are more than ready to be led towards moral damnation. Only Fanny Price, the poor relation who has achieved a better knowledge of what her adopted home stands for than its owners, retains a sense of proper values, and it is she who is entirely responsible for the salvation of Mansfield Park. By marrying Edmund Bertram, who inherits the Mansfield living, Fanny finally assumes a position of social authority close to that occupied by the earlier heroines. However, hers has been gained with much greater difficulty, and it is impossible to forget how close her society has come to disintegration.

The tone of *Emma* is much less sombre than that of *Mansfield Park*, but it does not mark a return to the effusive optimism of *Pride and Prejudice*. Whereas Mansfield Park is threatened by the loosening of traditional bonds, Highbury suffers from a tendency to be too well-ordered, and to oppose anything that threatens the *status quo*. This means that it has no problem resisting the corrupting influence of intruders like the manipulative Frank Churchill and the vulgarly bourgeois Mrs Elton, but is in real danger of experiencing the kind of total atrophy that can result from the refusal to accept necessary change. The salvation of the old society, however, once again proves to be possible. Emma Woodhouse and Mr Knightley both finally come to recognise the limitations of extreme conservatism, and enter into a marriage that promises the Highbury community more vigorous leadership than it experienced under Mr Woodhouse.

Having twice granted it a reprieve, Jane Austen seems no longer able to keep faith in the established order of things and, in *Persuasion*, she creates a world in which old certainties have finally crumbled.

Although the heroine, Anne Elliot, embodies within herself the best of traditional standards, she can do little to prevent Sir Walter Elliot's denial of responsibility and retreat from Kellynch Hall. Since Kellynch will not return to the Elliot family until inherited by William Walter Elliot, a man who unites the worst of middle-class materialism and aristocratic snobbery, there seems little hope for a moral revival of the landed interest. Thus, Anne must turn to the navy and the Musgroves, who represent, albeit in a somewhat idealised form, the bourgeoisie, because they, at least, remain true to such essential virtues as honesty, personal warmth and family feeling.

In the course of the nineteenth century, the conflict of values which Jane Austen describes turned into a struggle for power.[19] As the old order weakened and began to lose its authority, so those engaged in trade and industry made increasing demands that attention be paid to their values. They wanted England to be shaped in such a way as to foster free enterprise and social mobility; they wanted a society in which work and the acquisition of money were sources of prestige. Although Jane Austen died some seventeen years before the passing of the Great Reform Bill of 1832, which marked the first major step towards the institutionalising of middle-class values, there is plenty of evidence that she realised the tangible implications of changes in morality. For example, the inheritance of Norland by the essentially bourgeois John Dashwood, who regards his estate as an economic unit, is immediately followed by the cutting down of walnut trees, the building of greenhouses, and the purchase of additional profitable land (*Sense and Sensibility*, 225–6).

However, as a true child of her age, Jane Austen believed that the real conflict would be settled long before estates began to change hands or function, and that the fate of the landed classes depended on their ability to preserve the system of manners which buttressed their moral authority. Therefore, in Jane Austen's novels, the question of social morality and power is worked out largely in terms of a struggle between a Mr Knightley, who always employs manners to demonstrate his awareness of the needs of others, and a John Dashwood, who is polite only when it serves his own interests, or a Frank Churchill, who hides his real intentions behind a screen of good manners. The old order will survive only so long as Mr Knightley's manners are generally respected; once enough people accept the manners of John Dashwood or Frank Churchill then the selfish and acquisitive morality which they reflect will also be accepted.

Central though this equation between the polite behaviour of the individual and the moral health of the nation is to an understanding of Jane Austen's novels, there are only two occasions when she makes it explicit. The first of these is to be found in one of her earliest works, and, as is the case with most of the Juvenilia, the point is very nearly lost beneath the comic exaggeration of the surface. The incident in question occurs in 'Catherine' when the heroine argues with her aunt about the significance to be attached to what she considers to be a trivial breach of propriety:

> 'But I plainly see that every thing is going to sixes & sevens and all order will soon be at an end throughout the Kingdom.'
>
> 'Not however Ma'am the sooner, I hope, from any conduct of mine,' said Catherine in a tone of great humility, 'for upon my honour I have done nothing this evening that can contribute to overthrow the establishment of the kingdom.'
>
> 'You are Mistaken Child,' replied she: 'the welfare of every Nation depends upon the virtue of it's individuals, and any one who offends in so gross a manner against decorum & propriety is certainly hastening it's ruin. You have been giving a bad example to the World, and the World is but too well disposed to receive such.'   (*Minor Works*, 232–3)

In *Mansfield Park*, Edmund Bertram makes similar claims for manners during a discussion about the role of the clergy:

> And with regard to their influencing public manners, Miss Crawford must not misunderstand me, or suppose I mean to call them the arbiters of good breeding, the regulators of refinement and courtesy, the masters of the ceremonies of life. The *manners* I speak of, might rather be called *conduct*, perhaps, the result of good principles; the effect, in short, of those doctrines which it is their duty to teach and recommend; and it will, I believe, be every where found, that as the clergy are, or are not what they ought to be, so are the rest of the nation.   (93)

The fact that it is largely through manners that Jane Austen works out the question of social morality and power, brings us finally to the role played by the formal social occasion in her novels.

It is clear from Edmund Bertram's words quoted above that when Jane Austen speaks of manners, like Burke, she is embracing far more than the kind of strict etiquette that operates during a society's social rituals. Nevertheless, she realises that a context for exploring the whole of an individual's polite performance and for placing him within his group's moral hierarchy is provided only when an entire community is gathered together at a ball or a dinner. On no other occasion must the individual pay attention both to the informal and often improvised manners of everyday intercourse, and to the very demanding codes of the specific social ritual. Furthermore, since others are simultaneously engaged in the same activities, his relative moral worth is easily assessed. Thus, far from being mere illustrations of how a society amuses itself, the Bath balls in *Northanger Abbey* serve, amongst other things, to reveal the full differences in manners and hence morals between Catherine Morland's rival suitors, Henry Tilney and John Thorpe. At all levels, ranging from commonplace polite conversation about letter-writing or the pleasures of Bath to the etiquette of the dance invitation, Henry Tilney shows his concern with meeting Catherine's needs. Thorpe, on the other hand, whether holding forth about horses and dogs, or showing up late to claim a dance, consistently demonstrates that he is an egotistical boor. The Crown ball in *Emma* similarly demonstrates that Mr Knightley is superior to the Eltons. Their deficiencies are exposed in both great and small ways. Mr Elton, for example, offends grossly against propriety when he ostentatiously refuses to dance with Harriet Smith; his wife reveals her unworthiness by allowing herself a tiny but public smile of approval at her husband's conduct. Mr Knightley, by contrast, always demonstrates a concern for others, whether it be through the formal gesture of asking Harriet to dance, in order to save her further humiliation, or the informal one of taking Emma aside to offer a good-natured, but firm, critique of her behaviour (330–1).

Jane Austen's formal social occasions, however, do not yield up their full significance unless we recognise that she employs them almost invariably as initiation rituals. The initiation ritual, as Arnold van Gennep points out, is designed to test an individual's worthiness to pass from one relationship with his society to another.[20] However, the society too is implicitly under examination, because it is forced to articulate its values on these occasions. Jane Austen is acutely aware of the reciprocal nature of this process, and her novels progress through an intense interaction between the initiate, always a young woman struggling to make the transition from adolescence into adulthood, and her society, which has often lost sight of the very ideals which it is teaching through its rituals. The main emphasis of *Northanger Abbey*, for example, is placed inevitably on what the extremely naïve Catherine Morland has to learn. Nevertheless, it should not be forgotten that she gives her society some important reminders about the value of simplicity and openness. In *Mansfield Park*, on the other hand, it is the Mansfield community that is most in need of correction. Fanny Price, however, can still benefit from involvement in its rituals, which have a lot to teach her about the relationship between firm morality and charming display. Because this educational process, which takes place in all of Jane Austen's novels with the exception of *Persuasion*, is two-way, by the time the heroines achieve maturity and marry, not only have they proven themselves worthy of their society, but the society has proven itself worthy of them.

By examining formal social occasions, then, we can learn some important things about Jane Austen's social ideals, and about her sense of how well her society is living up to these ideals. We can also learn something about the shape of her novels, because the formal social occasion has an important structural role to play in each of them. Sometimes Jane Austen will pick up a tiny detail of ritual behaviour, such as the dance invitation in *Northanger Abbey*, or a pattern of movement between those involved in the ritual— Elizabeth Bennet's rejection of Darcy's approach and Edmund Bertram's oscillation between Fanny Price and Mary Crawford are examples that spring to mind—and will reiterate and develop it as a composer does a motif. At others, she will play off one formal social occasion against another. *Emma*, in particular, is built around contrasting scenes. And in all her novels she uses the visit to move her heroine between different moral universes which are then compared and contrasted. Rosings and Pemberley, for example, provide Elizabeth Bennet with two very distinct models of aristocratic behaviour and values.

However, generalisations will not take us far when it comes to considerations of form. The structure of any given work of art is unique because it develops out of the particular vision the author is trying to embody within that work of art. Therefore, to do justice to the unions of theme and form in Jane Austen's six completed novels, each must be considered as a separate entity. This will be the task of the body of my book, but I would like to sketch in here some of my main outlines, and to suggest how a consideration of Jane Austen's novels in sequence reveals not only a steady development in her view of society, but an ever more comprehensive grasp of the structural possibilities of the formal social occasion.[21] Even in her first novel, *Northanger Abbey*, Jane Austen demonstrates an awareness of some of the ways in which social rituals can be manipulated towards formal ends. The Bath episodes, which are made up of a series of fragmentary scenes that trace Catherine's endless movement from ballroom, to pump room, to theatre, and back to ballroom, appear at first sight to be rather chaotic. However, a sense of order emerges if attention is paid to the five balls and dance invitations around which Catherine's progress from social isolation to involvement with Henry Tilney is traced. A pattern of separation between Tilneys and Thorpes, and a motif involving the convention of the prior invitation, both of which underscore the process by which Catherine learns good judgement, further clarify the picture. Moreover, as in her mature novels, so in *Northanger Abbey*, Jane Austen establishes connections between the changes of location involved in visits and the moral development of the heroine. Catherine is removed from Fullerton to Bath so that she may learn something of the adult world, and then to Northanger Abbey so that she may achieve full maturity by working through, and eventually escaping from, her Gothic fantasies.

Sense and Sensibility is technically rather less satisfactory than *Northanger Abbey*. The scenes through which formal gatherings are presented again tend to be rather fragmentary, but this time there is little in the way of patterning. There is one pattern, based on visits to London and Cleveland, which embraces the whole novel. But apart from this there are only two partial patterns worthy of note. The first is constructed around contrasts between the formal behaviour of Elinor and Marianne, and the second around similar contrasts between Colonel Brandon and a number of other characters. Another approach is clearly needed to do justice to the many virtues of *Sense and Sensibility*. Nevertheless, a consideration of the consequences of the inadequate use of the formal social occasion in *Sense and Sensibility* is worthwhile, because it makes it possible to see why it serves such a valuable function in Jane Austen's other novels. For example, the extent to which our knowledge of Jane Austen's heroes and heroines depends upon their performance within the ritual context is made extremely clear if we consider her presentation of Edward Ferrars and Colonel Brandon. Both, but particularly

Edward, lack fully developed formal scenes in which to act, and as a consequence fail to convince us that they possess the worth their author claims for them.

Something of the full structural possibilities of the formal social occasion is revealed by *Pride and Prejudice*. In this novel Jane Austen creates a tripartite structure, each section of which is controlled by a different social ritual. The opening chapters are organised around four invitations to dance which create a pattern of approach and rejection emblematic of Darcy's frustrating relationship with Elizabeth. Then, in order to bring her heroine to an understanding of the aristocracy, Jane Austen takes Elizabeth to the diametrically opposed worlds of Rosings and Pemberley. Finally, the ritual of marriage takes control, and the unions of Wickham and Lydia, and Bingley and Jane, prepare the way for Darcy's marriage to Elizabeth.

Considerable as is the formal achievement of *Pride and Prejudice*, it is not the equal of *Mansfield Park*, in which Jane Austen makes much fuller use of the individual scene without sacrificing any of the intricacy of patterning to be found in the earlier novel. Episodes like the Sotherton visit and the theatricals are far more ambitious than anything that occurs in *Pride and Prejudice*, with the exception of the Netherfield ball. Yet they do not stand in isolation from one another, but are subsumed within larger structural units. Each of the main formal gatherings up to and including the theatricals, for instance, is characterised by the same central movement in which Edmund gravitates towards Fanny, only to be pulled away by the charms of Mary Crawford. In this novel, too, Jane Austen makes particularly telling use of changes in location. For example, visits to Sotherton and Portsmouth, places which are characterised by spiritual emptiness, lack of authority and loss of community, serve to dramatise the fate that awaits Mansfield Park should it yield itself up to the Crawfords.

Like *Mansfield Park*, *Emma* makes rich use of individual scenes, but again, they do not achieve their full impact unless we recognise their place within the overall pattern of formal social occasions. The Coles' dinner party and the Hartfield party, for instance, are set in ironic counterpoint to one another, in that the behaviour which Emma finds so offensive in Mrs Elton at Hartfield exactly parallels her own performance at the Coles'. Visits are also employed effectively. The trip to Donwell takes Emma to a place which serves as an appropriate background for the education in Highbury values she receives there. And it is equally fitting that she should commit her greatest offence against the standards of her community at Box Hill, the only location in the novel that falls outside the confines of the village.

Perhaps because it was never completely revised, and certainly because its subject matter forces Jane Austen to locate much of her action outside the formal context, *Persuasion* lacks the rich patterning of its immediate predecessors, and includes no scene equal to the Sotherton visit or the Crown Ball. Despite this artistic falling off, however, Jane Austen does make subtle use of both the occasional formal scene, like the Musgroves' evening party, and the more informal group gatherings, such as the walk to Winthrop, which particularly characterise this novel. Furthermore, visits to Uppercross, Bath and Lyme serve not only to reveal the very distinct 'little . . . commonwealths' (43) into which society has been fragmented, but also, through the contrasts established between the decadent Kellynch and Bath locations that frame the novel, and the fresh and almost naïve worlds of Uppercross and Lyme that occupy its central portions, provide the novel with its main structural framework.

In the chapters that follow the approach outlined in this introduction will be developed. By concentrating on one aspect of Jane Austen's art, her use of the formal social occasion, it becomes possible to look at her novels in a somewhat new way, and to cast some fresh light on their themes and structure.[22] This approach also helps demonstrate the unity of her artistic achievement. Read in sequence, the six novels reveal an evolving social vision and a continual search for an appropriate form within which to embody that vision. Thus it becomes evident that, ultimately, Jane Austen's greatness is to be found in a consideration of the complete body of her work rather than in any single novel, considerable as some of them are.

1 Northanger Abbey

In writing her first novel, Jane Austen was, not surprisingly, concerned to stake out her literary territory. Through an extended parody of Gothic conventions she announces that her fiction will deal with something other than cheap thrills and emotional self-indulgence. This has frequently been recognised.[1] What has not always been recognised is the extent to which she establishes what this something will be.[2] Although it does not treat the subject with as much subtlety as some of the later novels, *Northanger Abbey* is nevertheless very much about the connection between proper manners and a healthy society. Like them, too, it works out its thesis by following a young woman through the social rituals which test the quality of her polite performance, and which, once her worth has been proven, culminate in a marriage ceremony marking her assumption of a position of authority in the adult world.

The young woman in this case is Catherine Morland and her task is not so much to improve her own performance, which is always motivated by a keen concern for propriety, as to learn how to read the manners of others. This is not easy for Catherine because she tends to judge people according to the claims they make for themselves, rather than trust in what she observes of their actual behaviour. While this generosity ensures that she is in no danger of underrating excellent people like Henry and Eleanor Tilney, it also means that she is taken in too easily by villains ranging from the plausible General Tilney to the more or less implausible John and Isabella Thorpe. For Catherine Morland, then, growing up means in practical terms learning that distinctions must be drawn between the truly virtuous younger Tilneys and the Thorpes and General Tilney who only proclaim their virtue.

As in the later novels, also, Jane Austen takes care to establish the rank of her major characters, and, consequently, is able to embody within her study of their manners an argument about the relationship between virtue and social background. The sense of what is 'due to others' (101), which consistently motivates Catherine's

polite behaviour, and which characterises Henry Tilney's performance at the ball and as a clergyman, can be traced back to their
firm roots in the gentry. Similarly, the fact that the Thorpes are
middle class and that General Tilney likes to fancy himself an
aristocrat has a great deal to do with their particular deviations
from the norm of good manners. For John and Isabella Thorpe,
manners are a blind behind which they can pursue their materialistic goals, and for the General they are the servants of self-
glorification.

The maturity of *Northanger Abbey*, however, is most evident in
what Jane Austen does with the formal social occasion. In order to
provide contexts for Catherine's growth and for the revelation of the
moral worth of the people she encounters, Jane Austen draws on the
full range of Bath social activity. Catherine's daily round of visits to
the Pump-room, theatre and ballroom, her carriage rides, walks
and lunches easily qualify her as Jane Austen's most active heroine.
Only during the visit to Northanger Abbey does her pace lessen.
The brevity of the individual scenes and the rapid transitions
between scenes are intended to convey something of the excitement
and bustle of life in Bath, and they inevitably lend a certain air of
confusion to the first half of *Northanger Abbey*. This confusion,
however, is only apparent, because underneath the chaotic surface
are several patterns which provide the basis for the novel's structure
and point up some of its major themes.

I would like to concentrate on what I believe are the three most
important of these patterns. The first emerges from a number of
scenes which Jane Austen organises in such a way that the presence
of either the Thorpes or the Tilneys guarantees the absence or the
exclusion of the other family. The main purpose of the pattern is to
provide an emblematic equivalent for the moral exclusiveness of the
Thorpes and Tilneys, which is being revealed in the main body of
the action by their respective polite performances.[3] Catherine
Morland's ability to recognise only in part the appropriateness of
these separations helps to emphasise her lack of discrimination. The
second pattern, which is formed from several incidents involving
prior invitations, is kinder to Catherine, for it demonstrates that,
while 'her mind [may be] about as ignorant and uninformed as the
female mind at seventeen usually is' (18), nevertheless, she has a
well-developed sense of social duty, and is capable of learning from
experience. This pattern plays a particularly vital role in *Northanger
Abbey* because it helps to undo the impression, created accidentally

by the anti-Gothic satire of the novel's opening chapters, that Catherine is an unintelligent and poorly-educated person, completely unfitted to deal with the kind of subtle moral problems that Jane Austen poses for her. The prior invitation motif is complicated by its final appearance late in the novel. Earlier the convention was misused by the Thorpes, but now it is General Tilney who turns polite obligations to his own advantage. In this way Jane Austen links characters who are superficially very different. These two patterns are both subsumed within a third and larger pattern constructed around five invitations to dance and an invitation to visit Northanger Abbey, which mark out the main stages in Catherine's progression towards maturity. Beginning with her first evening at the Upper Rooms, during which she is socially excluded and does not receive even one invitation to dance, Catherine attends a number of balls in the course of which she learns to prefer Henry Tilney's invitations to John Thorpe's, but fails to see through Isabella Thorpe. The action is brought to its conclusion by the visit to Northanger Abbey, where Catherine's education is completed and she becomes discriminating enough to realise the truth about Isabella Thorpe and General Tilney.

Thus, unlike the more familiar entry through Jane Austen's Gothic satire, which tends to lead away from the novel's main concerns, a study of formal social occasions provides a very useful point of access into *Northanger Abbey*. The three patterns which it reveals emphasise the absolute moral distinctions that must be drawn between Henry and Eleanor Tilney and John and Isabella Thorpe, as well as the similarities between the Thorpes and General Tilney. In this way, the moral hierarchy to be decoded by Catherine is made clear to the reader. Furthermore, and most important, Catherine's own moral sense, which is concealed by the early Gothic satire and by her own naïvety, is fully demonstrated, and so is her ability to learn from experience and to develop towards maturity.

The frantic social activity in which Catherine Morland engages during the early days of her visit to Bath necessarily leads to the forming of a number of new acquaintances. In rapid succession she is introduced to Henry Tilney, Isabella Thorpe, James Thorpe and Eleanor Tilney. Yet, although all four are in Bath to enjoy the same public pleasures of Pump-room in the morning and theatre or ball in the evening, the Tilneys and the Thorpes are rarely present at the

same time. Even when they are, far from being united by their
common friendship with Catherine, they consistently exclude each
other. Thus, Catherine frequently discovers that by paying attention to one set of friends, she has lost an opportunity to enjoy the
other's company. The pattern first becomes evident during a visit to
the Pump-room. Catherine goes hoping to meet Henry Tilney, but
he is absent, and instead she makes the acquaintance of Isabella
Thorpe (31). A visit to the theatre in company with Isabella is
equally disappointing:

> Catherine was not so much engaged at the theatre that evening,
> in returning the nods and smiles of Miss Thorpe, though they
> certainly claimed much of her leisure, as to forget to look with an
> inquiring eye for Mr Tilney in every box which her eye could
> reach; but she looked in vain. Mr Tilney was no fonder of the
> play than the Pump-room.   (35)

During her next visit to the Upper Rooms, Catherine discovers that
by accepting John Thorpe's invitation to dance she has denied
herself a chance to partner Henry Tilney (54–5). And, after
lingering at the end of the dance to talk to Isabella Thorpe, she
returns to her seat to be informed by her aunt that she has thereby
just missed Henry Tilney: ' "Where can he be? " said Catherine,
looking round; but she had not looked round long before she saw
him leading a young lady to the dance' (58). Isabella's demands for
Catherine's attention also serve to cut short a promising introduction to Eleanor Tilney (56). The same pattern recurs when
Catherine chooses to ride with John Thorpe rather than attend the
Pump-room with Mrs Allen. On her return she discovers that she
has thereby lost an opportunity to walk with the Tilneys:

> 'Yes; we agreed to take a turn in the Crescent, and there we met
> Mrs Hughes, and Mr and Miss Tilney walking with her.'
>   'Did you indeed? And did they speak to you? '
>   'Yes, we walked along the Crescent together for half an
> hour.'   (68)

Up to this point the mutual exclusiveness of the two sets of friends
has been largely accidental, but there now follows a series of
incidents in which they make directly conflicting claims on
Catherine's attention. At her next ball, again in the Upper Rooms,

Catherine agrees to dance with Henry Tilney, thus angering John Thorpe who had anticipated being her partner: 'That is a good one, by Jove!—I asked you as soon as I came into the room, and I was just going to ask you again, but when I turned round, you were gone!—this is a cursed shabby trick!' (75). Similarly, two invitations to go walking with the Tilneys conflict directly with the Thorpes' plans that Catherine should accompany them on excursions to Bristol and Blaize Castle:

> 'To Bristol! Is not that a great way off?—But, however, I cannot go with you to-day, because I am engaged; I expect some friends every moment.' This was of course vehemently talked down as no reason at all.   (84)

And later:

> She had that moment settled with Miss Tilney to take their promised walk to-morrow; it was quite determined, and she would not, on any account, retract. But that she *must* and *should* retract, was instantly the eager cry of both the Thorpes.   (97)

Even though this pattern of exclusion pervades the Bath section of *Northanger Abbey*, it does not exceed its function. Indeed it serves several related functions. Above all, it is a metaphor for the main business of this part of the novel, which is the making of distinctions. Just as characters are literally kept apart, so it is the task of the author, the reader and Catherine Morland to separate them morally. The intensification of the pattern from accidental separations into direct conflict further suggests that once moral discriminations have been established, absolute choices must be made. The Tilneys and the Thorpes occupy distinct moral universes, and differences between them are of kind rather than degree.

To emphasise that each character must be viewed as a discrete being, Jane Austen introduces Catherine's four new acquaintances in turn, and allows each centre stage long enough for him or her to reveal the essential quality of his or her manners and morals. Henry Tilney, whom Catherine meets at the Lower Rooms, is the first to make an entrance. What is most notable about Tilney is his sophisticated manipulation of polite intercourse. By lightly mocking the clichés that characterise ballroom conversations, Tilney shows an awareness of the tendency of manners to degenerate into empty forms. Yet, at the same time, he manages his satiric comments in such a way that he is able to carry out his polite duty. Although asked with 'a simpering air' (26), Tilney's questions about the length of Catherine's stay in Bath and about her activities there nevertheless do serve the function of acquiring basic information and of setting his new acquaintance at ease. Subsequent mockery of journal-writing is similarly double-edged, in that Tilney uses it not only to ridicule convention but to uncover and encourage Catherine's basic good sense, to pay her a compliment on her dress, and to request her good opinion:

> 'Yes, I know exactly what you will say: Friday, went to the Lower Rooms; wore my sprigged muslin robe with blue trimmings—plain black shoes—appeared to much advantage; but was strangely harassed by a queer, half-witted man, who would make me dance with him, and distressed me by his nonsense.'
> 'Indeed I shall say no such thing.'
> 'Shall I tell you what you ought to say?'
> 'If you please.'
> 'I danced with a very agreeable young man, introduced by Mr King; had a great deal of conversation with him—seems a most extraordinary genius—hope I may know more of him. *That*, madam, is what I *wish* you to say.'   (26–7)

Further evidence of Henry Tilney's sophistication is provided by his conversation with Mrs Allen. Faced with an older and, as he soon realises, foolish woman, Tilney quickly modifies his tone. Although he cannot resist the temptation to introduce an element of mimicry into the earnest conversation about the cost and quality of muslin in which Mrs Allen engages him, Tilney controls it finely. Thus, Catherine understands him, but no offence is given to the butt of his humour:

> 'And pray, sir, what do you think of Miss Morland's gown?'
> 'It is very pretty, madam,' said he, gravely examining it; 'but I do not think it will wash well; I am afraid it will fray.'
> 'How can you,' said Catherine, laughing, 'be so——' she had almost said, strange.   (28)

Catherine concludes of Henry Tilney that 'he indulged himself a little too much with the foibles of others' (29). This is doubtless correct, but it fails to do full justice to his irony. By mocking Mrs Allen, Tilney is not simply amusing himself, he is also trying to teach Catherine that to talk to a young man about a topic in which he can scarcely be expected to have any interest is bad manners.

The polite performance of Isabella Thorpe, who now replaces Henry Tilney, is of a very different order. Whereas Tilney employs conversational trivialities to express his awareness of the needs of others, Isabella makes them serve as a source of self-glorification. The talk of balls, fashions, flirtation and quizzes which fills up Isabella's first meeting with Catherine in the Pump-room is aimed not at setting her new acquaintance at ease, but at revealing her own superiority:

> Miss Thorpe, however, being four years older than Miss Morland, and at least four years better informed, had a very decided advantage in discussing such points; she could compare the balls of Bath with those of Tunbridge; its fashions with the fashions of London; could rectify the opinions of her new friend in many articles of tasteful attire; could discover a flirtation between any gentleman and lady who only smiled on each other; and point out a quiz through the thickness of a crowd.   (33)

Isabella Thorpe's egotism is so overpowering that even expressions of friendship quickly turn into hymns of self-worship. Thus, while overtly engaged in defending Miss Andrews, 'one of the sweetest creatures in the world' (40), from the charge of insipidness, Isabella manages to give a lengthy account of her own virtues:

> There is nothing I would not do for those who are really my friends. I have no notion of loving people by halves, it is not my nature. My attachments are always excessively strong. I told Capt. Hunt at one of our assemblies this winter, that if he was to tease me all night, I would not dance with him, unless he would allow Miss Andrews to be as beautiful as an angel. The men think us incapable of real friendship you know, and I am determined to shew them the difference.   (40)

If the reader still has any doubts about where Isabella's real interests lie, they are dispelled when, in order to win further credit for being

Catherine's friend, she readily betrays Miss Andrews: 'you have so much animation, which is exactly what Miss Andrews wants, for I must confess there is something amazingly insipid about her' (41).

Despite these gross breaches of good manners, Isabella Thorpe is not entirely ignorant of the demands of propriety; she is simply unwilling to be guided by them. In order to close the gap between her theoretical knowledge of correct behaviour and her actual conduct, Isabella adopts a tactic which serves in fact only to emphasise it. When faced with a situation in which propriety is at odds with her own wishes, Isabella loudly proclaims her concern with good manners as a prelude to acting improperly. On one occasion, for example, she expresses great alarm at the prospect of being approached by two strange men who are supposedly staring at her across the Pump-room: 'For Heaven's sake! let us move away from this end of the room. Do you know, there are two odious young men who have been staring at me this half hour' (43). However, once they leave, she and the bemused Catherine Morland 'set off immediately as fast as they could walk, in pursuit of the two young men' (43).

John Thorpe, to whom we are next introduced, creates an even worse impression than his sister because he lacks the theoretical knowledge of good manners which gives at least a patina of propriety to her behaviour. Isabella is never guilty of the blatant rudeness which characterises the way John Thorpe greets his mother: ' "Ah, mother! how do you do?" said he, giving her a hearty shake of the hand: "where did you get that quiz of a hat, it makes you look like an old witch?" ' (49). Nor does she ride roughshod over the demands of propriety as he does when he tries to engage Catherine in a *tête-à-tête* carriage ride only moments after being introduced. In essentials, though, there is little to choose between brother and sister; both are completely selfish and egotistical. We may consider, for example, their first conversations with Catherine Morland. John Thorpe's self-serving intentions are blatant since, in choosing the speed of his horse and the quality of his gig as the means of demonstrating his own importance, he makes no pretence to be concerned with the needs of his audience: 'Hot! he had not turned a hair till we came to Walcot Church: but look at his forehead; look at his loins; only see how he moves; that horse *cannot* go less than ten miles an hour: tie his legs and he will get on. What do you think of my gig, Miss Morland? a neat one, is not it?' (46). Isabella is more subtle; balls and fashion are topics in which Catherine could be expected to take an interest. Consequently, she is able to give the impression that she is pursuing the proper ends of polite conversation. In reality, though, as we have already seen, her intentions are precisely the same as her brother's.

Finally, Eleanor Tilney makes her appearance, but it is only a brief one. The reader thus gains little first-hand experience of her polite performance, and has to rely on the author to place her within the novel's moral hierarchy. Jane Austen introduces her with the comment that, 'her air, though it had not all the decided pretension, the resolute stilishness of Miss Thorpe's, had more real elegance. Her manners shewed good sense and good breeding; they were neither shy, nor affectedly open' (55-6), and later confirms that she is a woman of 'simplicity and truth, and without personal conceit' (72).

Once each of Catherine's four new acquaintances has made his entrance it becomes evident why, as the separation motif suggests, absolute choices must be made between them. The polite performance of both Tilneys has been characterised by an acute sense of concern for others; the Thorpes' conduct has revealed that they acknowledge responsibilities only to themselves. There is no way in which such different approaches to experience can be reconciled and a clear sense of the consequences of trying to do so is given by the sequence of exclusions which occurs during the second ball in the Assembly Rooms. On this occasion, Henry, Eleanor, Isabella and John are all present, and Catherine tries to keep in touch with each of them. However, the obligation to dance with John Thorpe causes a separation from Henry Tilney, and Isabella Thorpe's claims on her attention pull her away from Eleanor Tilney. Finally, Catherine chooses to separate herself from John Thorpe, whose behaviour during their dance has been obnoxious, and is abandoned by Isabella. As a result, she ends the evening alone:

> The rest of the evening she found very dull; Mr Tilney was drawn from their party at tea, to attend that of his partner; Miss Tilney, though belonging to it, did not sit near her, and James and Isabella were so much engaged in conversing together, that the latter had no leisure to bestow more on her friend than one smile, one squeeze, and one 'dearest Catherine.'   (59)

The burden of this tableau and of the events which lead up to it is that, so long as she continues to pursue both friendships, Catherine is in danger of completely isolating herself. The selfish Thorpes will pull her away from the Tilneys, but they will then either prove to be unacceptable to her or will desert her when she ceases to be useful to them.

Failure to make choices, however, has implications that go even beyond the question of Catherine's personal happiness. This is suggested by the fact that Jane Austen draws her moral demarcation line, not between individuals but between families. Isabella and John, we are told, are the children of an attorney's widow from Putney; Henry and Eleanor are members of a landed family. And it is not hard to relate the virtues and vices of the Thorpes and the Tilneys to their social origins. Brought up in a world of business, the Thorpes are essentially acquisitive and self-seeking. Both cultivate what they take to be the ways of the gentry—John Thorpe by creating a persona based on an absurd combination of Squire Western [he has read *Tom Jones* (48)] and a Regency buck, and Isabella by striving for elegance and a façade of decorum. But it is not any admiration for the gentlemanly code of concern for others that inspires them to do this. Rather, they are simply preparing themselves for an attempt to enter a social realm they equate with wealth and prestige. The Tilneys, on the other hand, consistently reveal the kind of disinterestedness, breadth of vision, charm and grace, which were believed in the eighteenth century to be the prerogative of people fortunate enough to be removed from the hurly-burly of getting and spending, that is, of the landed classes. The choice which faces Catherine Morland, then, is important not just for herself but for her whole society. By aligning herself with the Tilneys she will be contributing to the continuing social leadership of an ethically sound group. By allowing herself to be influenced by the Thorpes, she will be helping to undermine the established order of things.

Catherine Morland's capacity for making these crucial moral choices is revealed by her role within the pattern of exclusion. At first, she fails completely to recognise that there is any logic behind the circumstances that are keeping her friends apart and, far from beginning to discriminate between them, she works to bring the Tilneys and Thorpes together. Thus, although they rarely come into close physical proximity, and are never part of the same circle, Catherine is often able to ensure that Henry, Eleanor, Isabella and John are united in spirit by making whichever of her friends is absent the subject of her thoughts or her conversation:

Here Catherine and Isabella, arm in arm, again tasted the sweets
of friendship in an unreserved conversation;—they talked much,
and with much enjoyment; but again was Catherine disappointed in her hope of re-seeing her partner. He was no where to
be met with . . . He must be gone from Bath . . . From the
Thorpes she could learn nothing . . . It was a subject, however,
in which she often indulged with her fair friend.   (35–6)

It is not a lack of moral sense that prevents Catherine from
recognising the inequality of her friends. Her own conduct is always
directed by a concern for 'what was due to others' (101). What
limits her is an excess of good will. Instead of striving to understand
the motives of another person by judging his actions, she either
supposes that his motives are similar to what would have been hers
in the same situation, or she accepts the interpretation that he or
another puts on his behaviour. Rather than trust what she sees of
John Thorpe's character, for example, she takes him to be the good
fellow posited by himself—'Oh! d—— it, when one has the means of
doing a kind thing by a friend, I hate to be pitiful' (47)—and by
her brother James: 'He is as good-natured a fellow as ever lived'
(50). Henry Tilney offers a definitive assessment of her mode of
judging:

How very little trouble it can give you to understand the motive
of other people's actions . . . With you, it is not, How is such a
one likely to be influenced? What is the inducement most likely to
act upon such a person's feelings, age, situation, and probable
habits of life considered?—but, how should *I* be influenced, what
would be *my* inducement in acting so and so.   (132)

However, Catherine does gradually begin to realise that to unite
is not always an appropriate course of action. Isabella Thorpe's web
of deception, transparent as it is, continues to be too much for her
throughout her visit to Bath. John Thorpe's behaviour, though, is so
objectionable that not even the benevolent Catherine can continue
to accept him at his own estimation. The process of disillusionment
is begun by his casual attitude towards their dance engagement, and
is completed by his performance during a subsequent carriage ride.
Whether frightening Catherine with accounts of his horse's high
spirits, or of the frailty of James Morland's carriage, probing into
the state of Mr Allen's finances, regaling her with his drinking

exploits, or generally engaging in 'talk, [which] began and ended with himself and his own concerns' (66), John Thorpe consistently shows himself to be without sensitivity towards the feelings or needs of his companion. By the end of the day Catherine is forced, very much against her will, to involve herself in the business of making judgements:

> Little as Catherine was in the habit of judging for her self, and unfixed as were her general notions of what men ought to be, she could not entirely repress a doubt, while she bore with the effusions of his endless conceit, of his being altogether agreeable. It was a bold surmise, for he was Isabella's brother; and she had been assured by James, that his manners would recommend him to all her sex.   (66–7)

This promising development is mirrored in the movement of the cotillion ball. At last, Catherine displays some sense of the need to exercise discrimination, and begins the evening determined to avoid John Thorpe and hoping to unite herself with Henry Tilney:

> She entered the rooms on Thursday evening with feelings very different from what had attended her thither the Monday before. She had then been exulting in her engagement to Thorpe, and was now chiefly anxious to avoid his sight, lest he should engage her again; for though she could not, dared not expect that Mr Tilney should ask her a third time to dance, her wishes, hopes and plans all centred in nothing less.   (74)

Albeit unwittingly, she also succeeds temporarily in the task which still faces her. Henry and Eleanor Tilney's company is so satisfying that, for one evening at least, neither her eyes nor her thoughts pursue Isabella Thorpe, and the exclusion which the novel seeks is for once complete: 'Of her other, her older, her more established friend, Isabella, of whose fidelity and worth she had enjoyed a fortnight's experience, she scarcely saw any thing during the evening' (81).

Catherine Morland's potential for moral growth, which is hinted at by her performance during the cotillion ball, is demonstrated more fully by the novel's second important structural pattern. This comprises four incidents involving prior invitations. The first occurs when Catherine turns down Henry Tilney's invitation to dance in favour of a previous engagement to John Thorpe; the second when she is persuaded to go on an excursion with the Thorpes and thereby fails to honour an obligation to walk with the Tilneys; the third when she refuses to break a subsequent engagement with the Tilneys despite pressure from the Thorpes; and the fourth when General Tilney uses a previous engagement to visit Lord Longtown as an excuse for dismissing Catherine from Northanger Abbey.

Catherine's second meeting with Henry Tilney in the Upper Rooms is particularly gratifying for her. Not only does his company free her from the 'state of humiliation' (53) created by John Thorpe's failure to honour their engagement to dance, but he again conducts himself in a witty and charming manner. Therefore, when Tilney asks her to dance, there is a good deal to persuade Catherine to accept. Yet she turns him down, and thereby reveals a keen sense that social obligations must take precedence over her own wishes. By agreeing to be John Thorpe's partner she has not simply secured her own enjoyment, but has incurred responsibilities towards him. The fact that Thorpe is not fulfilling his side of the bargain in no sense lessens Catherine's obligations. By her behaviour on this occasion, Catherine shows very clearly that even in the early stages of her introduction to the world she is by no means ignorant of, or uncaring about, the rules that govern it. However, what she doesn't understand is that some people lack her concern with propriety. A Henry Tilney may accept her refusal graciously, and doubtless will respect her all the more for it; but there are those who are not willing for their wishes to be frustrated.

As a result of this naïvety Catherine fares much less well on a later occasion when the roles are reversed, and the Thorpes are asked to stand down in favour of the Tilneys. Neither Isabella nor John Thorpe recognises that one has obligations to anyone except oneself and, therefore, they feel no compunction about trying to persuade Catherine to excuse herself from walking with the Tilneys so that she might ride with them. The delights of the country, the possibility of visiting Blaize Castle, the inadvisability of a walk when 'it is ancle-deep every where' (85), are all offered in rapid succession as reasons why Catherine should break her engagement. When all else fails, John Thorpe offers the flat lie that he saw the Tilneys leaving town. This, plus Mrs Allen's failure to offer proper guidance, persuades Catherine that it is proper to neglect her polite duty.

These two incidents demonstrate, then, that although Catherine is right thinking, there is little chance of her becoming an effective moral force unless she can overcome the naïve assumption that the whole world operates as she does. To show that Catherine is, in fact, capable of doing this, Jane Austen employs the simple device of repeating the situation in which her heroine has just failed. Once again Catherine is engaged to walk with the Tilneys, and once again the Thorpes propose an alternative outing. The pressure put on Catherine this time is intense. To counter her refusal to go back on her promise to the Tilneys, Isabella appeals to her loyalty as a friend, and then reproaches her for preferring Eleanor Tilney; her brother James accuses her of unkindness; and John Thorpe again tries to apply the *coup de grâce* of a lie. But Catherine is not to be distracted from her purpose. She judges Isabella to be 'ungenerous and selfish, regardless of every thing but her own gratification' (98); offers James only the compromise of joining the Thorpes' party on the next day; and is angered by John Thorpe's attempts to deceive.

Catherine triumphs here because she has realised that, far from being a matter of simply knowing the rules, propriety is something that must be pursued through a vigorous consideration of the moral implications of any given situation. The quality of the introspection in which she engages at the end of this painful encounter illustrates how far Catherine has progressed towards making a reality out of her new awareness:

> It was painful to her to disappoint and displease them, parti-
> cularly to displease her brother; but she could not repent her
> resistance. Setting her own inclination apart, to have failed a
> second time in her engagement to Miss Tilney, to have retracted
> a promise voluntarily made only five minutes before, and on a
> false pretence too, must have been wrong. She had not been
> withstanding them on selfish principles alone, she had not
> consulted merely her own gratification; *that* might have been
> ensured in some degree by the excursion itself, by seeing Blaize
> Castle; no, she had attended to what was due to others, and to her
> own character in their opinion.   (101)

Even this, though, does not end the matter for Catherine, and to gain further insight into the subtleties of her moral dilemma she goes so far as to question Mr Allen about it:

> She began . . . to doubt whether she had been perfectly right. A

sacrifice was always noble; and if she had given way to their entreaties, she should have been spared the distressing idea of a friend displeased, a brother angry, and a scheme of great happiness to both destroyed, perhaps through her means. To ease her mind, and ascertain by the opinion of an unprejudiced person what her own conduct had really been, she took occasion to mention before Mr Allen the half-settled scheme of her brother and the Thorpes for the following day.   (103–4)

The prior invitation pattern is completed by its reappearance late in the novel. Having been used earlier to show Catherine's capacity for moral growth, it now marks the point at which maturity is achieved. Of the various puzzles in manners that Catherine has to solve during the novel, the most difficult is that set by General Tilney. The polite surface he creates is much more convincing than either Isabella or John Thorpe's, and Catherine is driven to a Gothic interpretation of events to explain the uneasiness she feels in his company. Finally, though, her Gothic fantasies are shattered, and Catherine comes to accept completely that, in order to understand others, she must apply her knowledge of 'the manners of the age' (200). This revelation bears fruit in the way she responds when General Tilney dismisses her from Northanger Abbey on the grounds that he has recalled a prior invitation to visit Lord Longtown. Catherine is no longer tempted to provide a Gothic frame for this piece of villainy, or willing to accept the General's claims to propriety. Instead, she takes his behaviour for what it is: a piece of inexcusable rudeness:

From what it could arise, and where it would end, were considerations of equal perplexity and alarm. The manner in which it was done so grossly uncivil; hurrying her away without any reference to her own convenience, or allowing her even the appearance of choice as to the time or mode of her travelling; of two days, the earliest fixed on, and of that almost the earliest hour, as if resolved to have her gone before he was stirring in the morning, that he might not be obliged even to see her. What could all this mean but an intentional affront? By some means or other she must have had the misfortune to offend him.   (226)

The prior engagement motif, then, stresses Catherine Morland's ability to convert her impulse towards proper behaviour into the ordering principle of a life conducted amongst 'mixed characters' (200). By so doing, it corrects the most unpromising picture created by Jane Austen's decision to begin *Northanger Abbey* by dwelling on her limitations as a sentimental heroine. At times this satire against the creed of sensibility works well enough. The reader is not tempted, for instance, to think less well of Catherine because she is unable to 'learn or understand any thing before she was taught' (14). On the whole, though, it is handled rather clumsily, and the impression is conveyed that Catherine is mediocre, not only according to the standards of the sentimental novel, but also according to Jane Austen's standards.[4] Comments about Catherine's 'thin, awkward figure' and 'dark lank hair' (13), her lack of taste for a garden, her failure to learn the piano, and the reduction of her reading of Pope, Gray, Thomson and Shakespeare to a search for sentimental quotations, overpower the occasional hints that she is tractable, kind, sensible and soundly educated. Yet it is these hints that provide the basis for the character that emerges in the main body of the action. Judged in relation to the sentimental stereotype, Catherine Morland is certainly deficient. But for Jane Austen this is hardly a fault. We need only think of Isabella Thorpe and Marianne Dashwood to understand what she thinks of women who cultivate the creed of sensibility. Moreover, since Catherine Morland is not familiar with sentimental fiction before she visits Bath, her failure to live up to its ideals is hardly surprising. What really matters, as it does for all Jane Austen's heroines, is whether she is deficient when judged against the values of eighteenth-century English society. If attention is shifted away from the novel's Gothic satire to its more central study of manners and morals—and this is what the prior engagement motif helps us to do—there can be little doubt that Catherine Morland is an extremely worthy young woman who is acutely aware of the code of concern for others, and who has the capacity to live up to its demands.

While the main emphasis of the prior invitation motif falls on Catherine Morland, it also serves to bring into focus the very real similarities between the Thorpes and General Tilney.[5] Superficially, they have nothing in common. The Thorpes are low-bred, ill-mannered and blatantly self-seeking. General Tilney is an extremely refined man who always seems most concerned to meet Catherine Morland's needs. Yet they both offend against the prior invitation rule, the Thorpes by trying to make Catherine break a previous engagement, and General Tilney by inventing one to rid himself of Catherine's company. What this implies is that, contrary to all appearances, General Tilney is as selfish as the Thorpes. This revelation about General Tilney's character makes it possible to re-assess his earlier behaviour and to understand why Catherine is so troubled by his displays of kindness. Much as General Tilney may claim to be concerned with Catherine's well-being, a close exam-ination of what he actually does reveals that his primary aim is always, in fact, to demonstrate his own worth or to get his own way. For example, although he establishes 'anxiety for [Catherine's] comfort' (154) as the guiding principle of the journey to *Northanger Abbey*, General Tilney adopts a slow and inconvenient form of transportation in a 'fashionable chaise-and-four' (156) that does far more to enhance his prestige than to ensure his guest's physical or emotional ease. Later, at the Abbey, the General makes a great show of asking Catherine whether she prefers to be conducted around the grounds or the house, but actually more or less forces her to comply with his own wishes:

> Which would she prefer? He was equally at her service.—Which did his daughter think would most accord with her fair friend's wishes?—But he thought he could discern.—Yes, he certainly read in Miss Morland's eyes a judicious desire of making use of the present smiling weather.—But when did she judge amiss?   (176–7)

Despite the greater subtlety of his style, General Tilney behaves on these occasions very much as Isabella Thorpe does when she cloaks proclamations of her own importance within expressions of undying friendship, or when she conceals outrageously flirtatious behaviour beneath a mask of propriety. The effect of tying together characters of such different backgrounds within the same moral knot is to suggest that the life of the aristocrat is no more conducive to the development of proper values than that of the bourgeois. General Tilney, unlike his children who are firmly rooted in the gentry, likes to think of himself as a member of the nobility. He boasts of possessing 'as considerable a landed property as any private man in the county' (176), and lists among his friends the Marquis of Longtown and the Lady Frasers. Because of his aristocratic pretensions, Tilney, like most of the people of this class who appear in Jane Austen's novels, has become so bedazzled with his own importance as to forget that high rank is more a source of duty than prestige.

Although it has been convenient to separate out the two patterns already discussed, they should properly be seen as parts of a third and main pattern which encompasses the whole of the novel. This is constructed around a number of invitations to dance and an invitation to visit Northanger Abbey, and by following its progression, we can trace the main stages in the process by which Catherine develops her powers of discrimination, solves the problems of character with which she is faced, and is initiated into adulthood.

The transition from the protected environment of the family to the larger world of adulthood is never easy, and Jane Austen shapes the ball which Catherine attends shortly after arriving in Bath into a succinct emblem of the problems facing her heroine. To someone familiar only with the comfort of the family circle, the world of the ballroom appears at first to be chaotic and alien: 'But to her utter amazement she found that to proceed along the room was by no means the way to disengage themselves from the crowd; it seemed rather to increase as they went on' (21). Things have no discernible shape—Catherine can see 'nothing of the dancers but the high feathers of some of the ladies' (21)—and there is no place for newcomers, who consequently feel in danger of being 'torn asunder by any common effort of a struggling assembly' (21). Catherine, however, is quick to gain a sense of her world, and soon acquires 'a comprehensive view of all the company beneath her, and of all the dangers of her late passage through them. It was a splendid sight, and she began, for the first time that evening, to feel herself at a ball' (21). Her task now is to enter this new world, and to do this she must be invited to join in the dance. Unfortunately, Catherine lacks a proper guide, for her chaperone, Mrs Allen, knows no one and is consequently unable to secure her a partner. The exclusion which results is symbolised by the embarrassments of the tea interval:

When at last arrived in the tea-room, she felt yet more the awkwardness of having no party to join, no acquaintance to claim, no gentleman to assist them.—They saw nothing of Mr Allen; and after looking about them in vain for a more eligible situation, were obliged to sit down at the end of a table, at which a large party were already placed, without having any thing to do there, or any body to speak to, except each other.   (22)

Disappointing though the ball turns out to be, it does at least hint that better things are in store for Catherine. Her ability to find order beneath the surface confusion demonstrates her fitness for social intercourse, and the attention which she attracts as the crowds thin out suggests that she will not long be excluded from it: 'Every five minutes, by removing some of the crowd, gave greater openings for her charms . . . She *was* looked at . . . and with some admiration; for, in her own hearing, two gentlemen pronounced her to be a pretty girl.'   (23-4)

Sure enough, at her next ball, the master of ceremonies introduces Catherine to Henry Tilney, and she receives the invitation to dance which was so lacking before. Tilney, as I showed earlier, is a remarkable young man, able to combine a satiric spirit with a mature sense of decorum. The quality of Catherine's social performance is thus given a severe test. However, as we might expect from the ease with which she grasped the shape of things at her previous ball, she is up to the demands placed on her. Henry Tilney's bantering puzzles Catherine, but her temptation to laugh indicates that she takes it in the right spirit: 'Catherine turned away her head, not knowing whether she might venture to laugh' (26). Furthermore, by giving sensible answers to his facetious questions, Catherine forces Henry Tilney to take her seriously. Thus, after indulging himself in a series of exaggerated generalisations about female letter writing, none of which succeeds in leading Catherine away from her search for truth, Tilney finally pays her the compliment of a rational statement: 'I should no more lay it down as a general rule that women write better letters than men, than that they sing better duets, or draw better landscapes. In every power, of which taste is the foundation, excellence is pretty fairly divided between the sexes' (28). The extent to which Catherine has managed to impress Henry Tilney is revealed by his refusal to let her tell him a polite lie:

> Catherine coloured, and said, 'I was not thinking of any thing.'
> 'That is artful and deep, to be sure; but I had rather be told at once that you will not tell me.'
> 'Well then, I will not.'   (29)

It is evident from this exchange that Henry Tilney is already laying the groundwork for a more extended relationship based on an honesty and openness not often to be found in the general run of social intercourse.

Were the world made up of Henry Tilneys, Catherine Morland's initiation into adulthood would be easily effected. Unfortunately, it also contains Thorpes, and Catherine has a good deal to learn about people like them before she can claim to have grown up. Thus, whereas the ball at which she is introduced to Henry Tilney might be considered to represent society as it ought to be, one in which a young woman simply has to find a partner to be ensured of happiness, the next, at which the Thorpes are present, shows it as it is. In this world, it is not sufficient just to be invited to dance; one must choose the right partner. In other words, the transition from childhood involves not merely entering the adult world, but searching out those parts of it which can provide scope for the expression of sound morality and the pursuit of personal happiness. Because of Catherine's failure to recognise this, her third ball proves to be rather less pleasing than its predecessor. Even though she has doubts about John Thorpe from the beginning of their acquaintance, Catherine is nevertheless delighted when he asks her to dance, for her experience at her first ball has taught her the importance of having a partner. However, it quickly becomes apparent to her that 'to go previously engaged to a ball, does not necessarily increase either the dignity or enjoyment of a young lady' (55). John Thorpe causes Catherine great embarrassment by keeping her waiting for their dance and, worse still, she discovers that by accepting one invitation she is forced to turn down another that is more desirable. Even though Henry Tilney pays her polite attention while she is being neglected by Thorpe, Catherine is forced to refuse his invitation to dance because of her previous engagement. Catherine's mortification is completed by Thorpe's behaviour when he finally puts in an appearance. No apology is forthcoming, and he bores her with talk of horses and dogs. Although its immediate effects are unpleasant, this is a valuable experience for Catherine because it teaches her something of the need to exercise discrimination when choosing a partner. She is not given another chance during the evening to dance with Henry Tilney, but, by turning down John Thorpe's next invitation, she shows that she has begun to learn that no partner is better than the wrong one:

'Well, Miss Morland, I suppose you and I are to stand up and jig it together again.'

'Oh no; I am much obliged to you, our two dances are over; and, besides, I am tired, and do not mean to dance any more.'   (59)

Unfortunately, these emerging powers of discrimination do not extend to Isabella Thorpe. Isabella's behaviour throughout the evening is stamped with her usual selfishness and impropriety. She promises, for example, to delay her entry into the dance until Catherine's partner returns, but three minutes is as long as she can put the needs of another ahead of her own wishes. Thinly disguising her selfishness by claiming to have been overcome by James Morland's persuasion, she abandons Catherine and heads into the dance: 'My dear creature, I am afraid I must leave you, your brother is so amazingly impatient to begin' (52). Catherine is a little disappointed at this desertion, but shows no signs of penetrating Isabella's façade of friendship. Later in the evening, Isabella expresses great interest in talking about Eleanor and Henry Tilney. However, she quickly becomes bored with a topic that does not relate directly to herself and diverts attention to her own relationship with James Morland:

'Oh! heavens! You don't say so! Let me look at her this moment. What a delightful girl! I never saw any thing half so beautiful! But where is her all-conquering brother? Is he in the room? Point him out to me this instant, if he is. I die to see him. Mr Morland, you are not to listen. We are not talking about you.'   (57)

Even when faced with such gross hypocrisy Catherine experiences no more than 'a little suspicion at the total suspension of all Isabella's impatient desire to see Mr Tilney' (57).

Catherine Morland, then, is not particularly successful in the business of choosing partners, and this results in a most unsatisfactory ball. Nevertheless, the evening is by no means a total loss for, besides learning something from dancing with John Thorpe, she behaves so well in her brief encounters with Henry and Eleanor Tilney, that they surely make some progress towards choosing her. The fact that Henry Tilney lingers near Catherine's seat hoping for another opportunity to ask her to dance shows that he recognises her first rejection as a mannerly act rather than a personal insult. And, by displaying 'the real delicacy of a generous mind' (55) to Eleanor Tilney, Catherine starts their relationship off in a promising way.

As a result of her experience on this occasion, Catherine is able to do somewhat better at the cotillion ball. John Thorpe again belongs to Catherine's party, and so she is guaranteed someone with whom to dance. Simply to have a partner, however, is no longer enough for Catherine. By dancing with Thorpe she would be subjecting herself to the attentions of a man whom she dislikes and would be losing the opportunity to find a better partner. Therefore, she does her best to avoid Thorpe, in the hope that Henry Tilney might appear and engage her himself: 'As soon as they were joined by the Thorpes, Catherine's agony began; she fidgetted about if John Thorpe came towards her, hid herself as much as possible from his view, and when he spoke to her pretended not to hear him' (74). As it turns out, Thorpe is dilatory and by the time he comes over to Catherine, she has been claimed by Henry Tilney. Nevertheless, by acting in this way, Catherine has taken a considerable risk. Should she have been successful in avoiding Thorpe, but not been sought out by Tilney, she would have found herself completely isolated. This, however, is a consequence Catherine must be willing to suffer if she is to retain her moral integrity.

Catherine is richly rewarded for her polite heroism. In as decisive a way as is possible for a woman, she has made clear her preference for Henry Tilney, and he responds, albeit in his usual indirect and ironic style, by suggesting that their temporary partnership in dance might be translated into the more permanent one of marriage. Under the guise of constructing a series of playful comparisons between dancing and matrimony, Henry Tilney manages to make claims on Catherine and to define what he would expect of her as a wife:

> We have entered into a contract of mutual agreeableness for the space of an evening, and all our agreeableness belongs solely to each other for that time. Nobody can fasten themselves on the notice of one, without injuring the rights of the other. I consider a country-dance as an emblem of marriage. Fidelity and complaisance are the principal duties of both.   (76)

The personal application of these remarks is underlined when, in rounding off his metaphor, Tilney pushes Catherine to admit that she is interested in him:

'You totally disallow any similarity in the obligations; and may I
not thence infer, that your notions of the duties of the dancing
state are not so strict as your partner might wish? Have I not
reason to fear, that if the gentleman who spoke to you just now
were to return, or if any other gentleman were to address you,
there would be nothing to restrain you from conversing with him
as long as you chose?'

'Mr Thorpe is such a very particular friend of my brother's,
that if he talks to me, I must talk to him again; but there are
hardly three young men in the room besides him, that I have any
acquaintance with.'

'And is that to be my only security? alas, alas!'

'Nay, I am sure you cannot have a better; for if I do not know
any body, it is impossible for me to talk to them; and, besides, I do
not *want* to talk to any body.'   (77–8)

Tilney's wisdom in choosing Catherine as his partner is borne out by
her subsequent conversational performance which reveals her to be
a cut above the usual run of Bath society:

'Oh! who can ever be tired of Bath?'

'Not those who bring such fresh feelings of every sort to it, as
you do. But papas and mammas, and brothers and intimate
friends are a good deal gone by, to most of the frequenters of
Bath—and the honest relish of balls and plays, and every-day
sights, is past with them.'   (79)

By the time Catherine attends her next and last ball, there is no
longer any question about who will ask her to dance and whom she
will accept. Just as he was 'born off by the resistless pressure of a long
string of passing ladies' (76) after unsuccessfully trying to establish a
prior claim to Catherine at the cotillion ball, so John Thorpe has
been carried beyond her sphere of social possibilities. Henry Tilney
is now Catherine's only possible partner, and the previously
troublesome business of choosing is dismissed in half a sentence:
'Miss Tilney took pains to be near her, and Henry asked her to
dance' (131). Unfortunately, though, the powers of discrimination
which have produced this satisfactory situation are still not
sufficiently well-developed to enable Catherine to grasp the truth
about Isabella Thorpe. In spite of Isabella's repeated displays of
bad manners and selfishness, Catherine continues to accept naïvely

her claims to propriety, as is evident on this occasion. Supposedly heartbroken by her temporary separation from James Morland, Isabella attends the ball only on the condition that she not be expected to dance. Yet, once an attractive partner emerges, in the shape of the handsome and rich Captain Tilney, she changes her mind at once. Catherine is naturally puzzled by the incongruity between her friend's intentions and behaviour. Nevertheless, Isabella is easily able to satisfy her, and at the same time to increase her own importance, by explaining that she gave in to Captain Tilney rather than continue to suffer the 'fine speeches and compliments' (134) by means of which he was trying to persuade her to accept him.

An impasse has been reached, then. By his repeated invitations to dance, Henry Tilney has firmly announced his interest in forming a more permanent partnership. But Catherine seems incapable of developing the level of maturity necessary if she is to deserve this final invitation to marry. She has seen through John Thorpe, but is almost as ignorant of Isabella's defects as when they first met. As it turns out, one more invitation is needed to break through the impasse. By asking her to visit Northanger Abbey, General Tilney provides Catherine with a new set of problems in judgement, and it is directly as a result of solving these that she acquires insight into Isabella Thorpe's character.

Catherine feels a slight sense of unease during all her encounters with General Tilney in Bath, but fails to realise that it derives from the General's cleverly concealed selfishness and concern with his own importance. This is not surprising, because it would need powers of discrimination far greater than those possessed by a young woman who cannot even penetrate Isabella Thorpe's disguises to blame the awkwardness of luncheon and breakfast engagements at Pulteney Street on someone who is 'perfectly agreeable and good-natured, and altogether a very charming man,' and 'tall and handsome, and Henry's father' (129). Problems of interpretation, however, become even more difficult at Northanger Abbey, because the tension created by General Tilney merely feeds the feelings of suspense already stirred up in Catherine as a result of visiting a Gothic abbey. For instance, the little piece of manipulation by which General Tilney induces Catherine to walk in the grounds rather than explore the Abbey naturally causes his daughter some embarrassment. However, because she is so ready to accept the General's claims to be concerned with her pleasure, Catherine is incapable of recognising the real source of Eleanor's discomfort. Instead, she begins to suspect mysteries of a Gothic nature: 'Why was Miss Tilney embarrassed? Could there be any unwillingness on the General's side to shew her over the Abbey? The proposal was his own. And was not it odd that he should *always* take his walk so early?' (177). A similar process is at work later when, rather than accept that General Tilney's refusal to hang his wife's picture in his own room derives from a fastidious objection to its quality as a work of art, Catherine takes it as evidence of the guilty workings of a murderer's conscience:

> Catherine attempted no longer to hide from herself the nature of the feelings which, in spite of all his attentions, he had previously excited; and what had been terror and dislike before, was now absolute aversion. Yes, aversion! His cruelty to such a charming woman made him odious to her. She had often read of such characters; characters, which Mr Allen had been used to call unnatural and overdrawn; but here was proof positive of the contrary.   (181)

Oddly enough, then, because she is unwilling to acknowledge General Tilney's real and very petty defects, Catherine ends up believing him to be guilty of a most hideous crime. As a consequence of straying so far beyond the bounds of reason, Catherine at last receives the shock necessary to make her realise the inadequacy of her method of judging. Henry Tilney's discovery that she has been thinking his father a wife-murderer fills her with such shame that she comes firmly down to earth, and from that point on accepts that the only way to learn the truth about people is to study their manners and conduct. Thus, in her reading of the letter which she receives shortly afterwards from Isabella Thorpe, Catherine pays attention, not to its protestations of friendship and propriety, but to its 'inconsistencies, contradictions, and falsehood', and refuses to be taken in by such 'a strain of shallow artifice' (218). Neither can General Tilney deceive her any more. For all his claims to have remembered a previous engagement, Catherine recognises that to dismiss her from Northanger Abbey in such a fashion is a complete breach of good manners.

The way has now been prepared for the novel's final invitation. Henry Tilney goes against his father's wishes and follows Catherine to Fullerton, where he asks her to marry him. By so doing he acknowledges that Catherine is finally worthy to be admitted into the adult world. Furthermore, he forms a bond that promises well for the future of his society. The Thorpes have been defeated, General Tilney has been reduced to impotence, and, as is suggested by Henry and Catherine's occupancy of the Woodston Parsonage, the spiritual leadership of the community has come to rest firmly in the hands of two people who have demonstrated their commitment to the gentlemanly ideal of concern for others.

Northanger Abbey, then, cannot be dismissed as a mere apprentice novel. It may bear affinities with the essentially satirical Juvenilia, but it has far more in common with the works of Jane Austen's maturity, and the approach adopted here will work just as well with *Pride and Prejudice, Mansfield Park* and *Emma*. Having discovered that the formal social occasion could provide her with a means of binding together theme and form, Jane Austen continued to make extensive use of it in all her later novels. Therefore, although her social vision matures and gradually changes, and her techniques become more intricate, *Northanger Abbey* is the germ out of which the whole of Jane Austen's achievement grows.

2 Sense and Sensibility

In *Northanger Abbey* the frequent meetings between Henry Tilney and Catherine Morland in the ballroom at Bath and during the visit to the Abbey are central to our comprehension of the novel's main issues. Without them, the reader would be hard pressed to understand the characters of Catherine and Henry, their relationship, Catherine's education in manners, or the social implications of their marriage. Considerable weight is also placed on the courtship aspects of the formal social occasion in all the novels subsequent to *Sense and Sensibility*, each of which is structured in part around the successful relationship between hero and heroine, and the abortive courtships that often prepare the way for this final proper union. In *Sense and Sensibility*, however, none of Elinor Dashwood's few significant encounters with her future husband, Edward Ferrars, takes place within the formal context and, while they often attend the same functions, Marianne has little to do with Colonel Brandon, the man whom she eventually marries. Neither do courtships with people other than their eventual partners much occupy the major characters. Marianne Dashwood is involved briefly with Willoughby, and we experience Edward Ferrars' relationship with his secret fiancée, Lucy Steele, only through retrospective summary. This does not automatically mean that there is anything wrong with *Sense and Sensibility*. Only the critic who has become infatuated with his thesis would condemn a work of literature simply because it does not conform with the pattern that he is tracing. Nevertheless, since *Sense and Sensibility* ends, as the other novels do, in a marriage, or in this case, marriages which have important implications for the individual and the society, it is reasonable to enquire how, in the absence of courtship, Jane Austen prepares the ground for her final statement. The Barton–Delaford community which is established at the end of the novel is called upon to carry a heavy symbolic weight, since it evolves from the union of the mature heroines with two of society's spiritual and social leaders, the clergyman, Edward Ferrars, and the landed gentleman, Colonel Brandon. It will fail to convince, however, unless Jane Austen has found ways of demonstrating the worth of her four characters, of the relationships between them, and of their manners and morals.

Part of the role of the courtship plot is taken over by a detailed presentation of Elinor Dashwood's inner life and of her intimate conversations with Marianne.[1] Consequently, the reader is given a thorough knowledge of Elinor's character, some sense of how she should respond to Marianne, Edward Ferrars and Colonel Brandon, all of whom fall under her scrutiny, a partial dramatisation of Marianne, and information about the temperamental and philosophical differences between the sisters. However, there is no similar shift from the outer world to the inner in Jane Austen's characterisation of Colonel Brandon and Edward Ferrars. Their minds remain closed off to the reader and he can know them only through their polite behaviour. Therefore, they need roles which will perform a function similar to that of the active suitor in Jane Austen's other novels. These they are not given; Edward Ferrars is too shy to involve himself in society at all, and Colonel Brandon's low spirits frequently force him into the background. As a result, neither is adequately realised as a character.[2] To believe in Edward the reader must put a good deal of faith in Elinor's claim that he possesses 'innate propriety' (19), and must assume that, once he has been freed from debilitating idleness by the choice of a profession, and from secrecy by the revelation of his clandestine engagement, he will be able to develop 'easy and graceful' (94) manners. Colonel Brandon is not such a hopeless case. By offering Edward Ferrars a living, and by agreeing to bring Mrs Dashwood to Marianne's sickbed, he gives very practical demonstrations of his awareness of the needs of others and of his ability to meet these needs. However, he rarely exerts himself within the polite context, and unless the reader is alert to incidents like the one in which he intervenes to save Elinor from Margaret's teasing (61–2), there is some danger that Colonel Brandon also will disappear from the novel.[3]

Jane Austen has even less success in finding alternative ways of performing the other functions of formal courtship. Given her failure to dramatise the two male characters, it would have been very difficult for her to come up with a way of developing relationships between the heroes and heroines strong enough to justify the almost idyllic happiness claimed for the marriages in which the novel culminates. In fact, though, she almost completely ignores the problem. Edward Ferrars' contacts with Elinor are limited to occasional private conversations which, revealing though they are, do not begin to give any sense of a complete relationship, and Marianne's involvement with Colonel Brandon, which commences as the novel ends, is passed over in a few sentences (378–9).

Neither does Jane Austen manage to demonstrate that her major characters have a grasp of the full implications of manners. As a result the kind of connection established in *Northanger Abbey*, between polite performance, the moral growth of the individual, and the health of society, is simply not to be found in *Sense and Sensibility*; and the value of the Barton-Delaford community is further undermined. Colonel Brandon and Edward Ferrars, as already indicated, have deficiencies of temperament which prevent them fulfilling their polite potential. Marianne Dashwood, on the other hand, disqualifies herself from engaging in polite intercourse for much of the novel because she believes that decorum is a form of hypocrisy: 'I have been too much at my ease, too happy, too frank. I have erred against every common-place notion of decorum; I have been open and sincere where I ought to have been reserved, spiritless, dull, and deceitful' (48). A near fatal illness finally makes Marianne realise that she has given others 'less than their due' (346), and that she should 'practise the civilities, the lesser duties of life, with gentleness, and forbearance' (347). However, the novel ends without any demonstration of how she puts her new beliefs into practice.[4]

Unlike Brandon, Ferrars, and Marianne, Elinor Dashwood is able and willing to engage herself in society, and never neglects even the most tiresome of polite duties: 'Elinor set out by herself to pay a visit, for which no one could really have less inclination, and to run the risk of a *tête-à-tête* with a woman, whom neither of the others had so much reason to dislike' (294). However, Elinor's social life is conducted almost entirely in the company of good-natured fools like Sir John Middleton or cold materialists like John Dashwood and, therefore, her good manners can rarely be more than a means of concealing her true reaction to the stupidity or cynicism of her companions. Jane Austen comments, for example, of her response to Lucy Steele's deliberately provocative hints about Edward Ferrars, that 'Elinor perfectly understood her, and was forced to use all her self-command to make it appear that she did *not*' (217–18). Later, rather than expose the stupidity of Robert Ferrars' babblings about his role in organising a dance at Lady Elliot's cottage, 'Elinor agreed to it all, for she did not think he deserved the compliment of rational opposition' (252).

To behave like this is not, as I will suggest in more detail later, immoral. There is some value in fostering even an illusion of social harmony and, by avoiding the alienation for which Marianne strives, Elinor provides herself with opportunities 'to see and observe' (118) and thus to engage in the vital business of judging others by 'an impartial consideration' (336) of their behaviour. As she argues in a conversation with Colonel Brandon, if 'one is guided by what they [people] say of themselves,' or by 'what other people say of them, without giving oneself time to deliberate and judge,' the result is likely to be 'a total misapprehension of character' (93). However, manners should be more than 'polite lies'[5] and Elinor gets few chances to demonstrate this. One of these occurs during a visit to the John Dashwoods when, not content for once simply to avoid agreeing with her step-brother, Elinor manoeuvres within the framework of polite convention so as to assert her own values:

> 'We think *now*'—said Mr Dashwood, after a short pause, 'of *Robert's* marrying Miss Morton.'
> Elinor, smiling at the grave and decisive importance of her brother's tone, calmly replied,
> 'The lady, I suppose, has no choice in the affair.'
> 'Choice!—how do you mean?'—
> 'I only mean, that I suppose from your manner of speaking, it must be the same to Miss Morton whether she marry Edward or Robert.'
> 'Certainly, there can be no difference; for Robert will now to all intents and purposes be considered as the eldest son.'
> (296–7)

The ironic point is, of course, completely lost on John Dashwood. Nevertheless, it has been made and is available to anyone willing to pay close attention to Elinor. However, she conducts herself like this too infrequently for her polite performance to have any real influence on the behaviour of others or to contribute to the moral health of society.

Because Elinor's manners usually serve a purely defensive function, and because the other major characters are either unable or unwilling to engage themselves in polite intercourse, the Barton–Delaford community appears to evolve in isolation from its society rather than by establishing authority over it. Few attempts are made either to influence or to challenge the novel's disruptive forces, and as a result the bourgeois materialists, John and Fanny Dashwood and Lucy Steele, do not suffer exposure and humiliation as Isabella Thorpe does, and the pseudo-aristocratic Mrs Ferrars retains a control that is denied to General Tilney. Whereas the Thorpes disappear into oblivion at the end of *Northanger Abbey*, and General Tilney must seek reconciliation with a son who has denied his authority, the London circle of Mrs Ferrars, Robert and Lucy Ferrars, and the John Dashwoods not only remains intact, but is placated by yet another of Elinor's polite lies. Thus, when Edward argues, quite reasonably, 'I know of no submission that *is* proper for me to make', Elinor, who is very concerned about his financial prospects, replies

'You may certainly ask to be forgiven . . . because you have offended;—and I should think you might *now* venture so far as to profess some concern for having ever formed the engagement which drew on you your mother's anger . . . And when she has forgiven you, perhaps a little humility may be convenient while acknowledging a second engagement, almost as imprudent in *her* eyes, as the first.'   (372)

Because of Jane Austen's failure to find objective correlatives to replace the courtship ritual, there is, then, a considerable discrepancy between what is claimed for Barton–Delaford and what the reader actually experiences. There can be no doubt of what Jane Austen intended. Barton–Delaford is supposed to be a core of mature relationships, good manners and sound morality that will radiate out through the society. Elinor's eventual success in convincing Marianne of the necessity of operating within the social context; the many clear statements made about the moral integrity of the four major characters; and the happiness claimed for their marriages, all contribute to this conclusion. Yet, because the male characters are so poorly presented, because the two love relationships are so inadequately defined, and because there are so few occasions when polite display actively reinforces sound morality, Barton–Delaford emerges as something rather like Bleak House, a place to which a small group of good but powerless people retreat rather than continue to expose themselves to a corrupt world.

By examining the role of the formal social occasion further, I cannot hope to remove entirely the impression that *Sense and Sensibility* is a harbinger of Victorian alienation. The novel is, as I have already tried to indicate, radically flawed, and its faults extend into a rather unsatisfactory deployment of social rituals. There are a great many formal occasions in *Sense and Sensibility*—the Middletons' gregariousness ensures this—but very few are fully presented, and they only occasionally perform a structural function.[6] Three patterns do emerge, though, which deserve attention. The first is constructed around a series of comparisons between the polite behaviour of Elinor and Marianne, and serves to emphasise that, for all its limitations, Elinor's approach to experience is preferable to her sister's. The second is based on a series of visits which establish four different social milieus. All are rather imperfect, but moral distinctions can be drawn between them if a comparison is made of the different styles of social intercourse that occur in each. Since Elinor recognises these distinctions, while Marianne ignores them, further justification is provided for the energy she puts into making judgements and establishing discriminations. The third pattern is again built on comparisons, this time between Colonel Brandon and a number of other characters, and reveals that Brandon's grasp of his social responsibilities is superior to that of almost any other member of his circle. The sum total of these three patterns is to reinforce the novel's conclusions. Elinor Dashwood's wisdom and sound morality are confirmed, and the reader can therefore trust a little more in the validity of a world into which her judgements often provide the only access; Marianne Dashwood's limitations are clearly exposed, thus removing the temptation to believe that she can offer any alternative to Elinor's values; and Colonel Brandon emerges as a rather more adequate symbol of authority.

Elinor Dashwood's refusal to express her dislike of social mediocrity has created a good deal of sympathy for Marianne Dashwood and for the more 'sincere' approach she derives from the creed of sensibility.[7] However, if account is taken of a number of incidents in which Jane Austen directly compares the social performances of the two sisters, there can be little doubt that Elinor's is superior. Though she does not believe she has any obligation to attend to the needs of fools and villains, Marianne prides herself on her concern for those she loves. Yet it is these loved ones who usually suffer most as a result of her refusal to contain her feelings or to be polite to people she dislikes. Thus, by striving for openness and honesty Marianne tends to produce results very different from what was intended. Marianne also has enormous faith in her powers of judgement, so much so that she cannot imagine ever being required to change her mind: 'At my time of life opinions are tolerably fixed. It is not likely that I should now see or hear anything to change them' (93). Her failure to engage in polite intercourse, however, frequently causes her to make inaccurate assessments of people. Elinor Dashwood, on the other hand, relates to society in such a way that she is consistently able to accomplish her ends. By pursuing a policy of 'general civility' (94), she ensures that she is always able to meet the needs of others, and by remaining within the social context, she ensures that she is well placed to make the impartial observations on which her generally accurate judgements are based.

We might take as our starting point an incident which epitomises the different social attitudes of the two sisters. Neither is willing to become involved in the game of Casino with which Lady Middleton proposes to enliven an evening at Barton Park. Marianne knows she will be bored and prefers to play the piano; Elinor has urgent reasons for wanting to talk to Lucy Steele. Their ways of escaping are characteristic. Marianne bluntly proclaims her dislike of card-playing, and so offends Lady Middleton:

'Your ladyship will have the goodness to excuse *me*—you know I detest cards. I shall go to the piano-forté; I have not touched it since it was tuned.' And without farther ceremony, she turned away and walked to the instrument.

Lady Middleton looked as if she thanked heaven that *she* had never made so rude a speech.   (144–5)

Elinor is much more cunning. Playing on Lady Middleton's affection for her children, she offers to give up her own pleasure and help Lucy finish a basket for little Annamaria. Jane Austen's sympathies are with Elinor: 'Elinor joyfully profited by the first of these proposals, and thus by a little of that address, which Marianne could never condescend to practise, gained her own end, and pleased Lady Middleton at the same time' (145). Many readers, on the other hand, can see little value in pandering to Lady Middleton, and prefer Marianne's honesty.

The limitations of this honesty become apparent, though, in three other polite incidents. While entertaining Edward Ferrars at Barton cottage, both Elinor and Marianne are intrigued by the plait of hair they see in his ring. Elinor's interest is particularly intense because she believes it to be her own hair; Marianne is merely curious. Elinor, however, refrains from comment because she is not certain of her facts; Marianne, on the other hand, simply expresses what is on her mind: ' "I never saw you wear a ring before, Edward," she cried. "Is that Fanny's hair? I remember her promising to give you some. But I should have thought her hair had been darker" ' (98). As a result she comes close to exposing Edward's secret engagement, and causes him considerable embarrassment. This was not at all Marianne's intention because she is, in fact, very fond of Edward, and she is upset to discover that she has hurt him: 'Marianne spoke inconsiderately what she really felt—but when she saw how much she had pained Edward, her own vexation at her want of thought could not be surpassed by his' (98). Here, then, is an incident in which honesty and spontaneity fail to produce their desired effect, and thus prove to be an inadequate basis for communication.

Lack of discretion also leads Marianne astray during a dinner at the John Dashwoods. Mrs Ferrars' behaviour towards Elinor throughout the evening is disgraceful, and culminates in a rude refusal to look at the screens she has painted: ' "Hum"—said Mrs Ferrars—"very pretty,"—and without regarding them at all, returned them to her daughter' (235). Elinor has little respect for Mrs Ferrars and so is not hurt by her rudeness. In fact, she is rather amused to observe the attention Mrs Ferrars pays to Lucy Steele who, as Edward's actual fiancée, has committed the very offence of which she is suspected herself. Elinor's complaisance on this occasion, then, does not merely reflect an unwillingness to disturb social harmony, but constitutes a very real statement of indifference. Marianne, however, does not stop to consider what Elinor might actually be thinking and, assuming that she must be mortified, violently rebukes Mrs Ferrars. Consequently, as she did with Edward, Marianne causes pain to the very person with whose comfort she is concerned. 'Elinor was much more hurt by Marianne's warmth, than she had been by what produced it' (236).

Perhaps the most conclusive example of Marianne's inability to produce the results she desires is given by her behaviour during a meeting with Elinor, Edward Ferrars and Lucy Steele. This scene is one in which Elinor fares particularly well, since she takes charge and begins a polite performance designed to alleviate a very awkward situation:

But Elinor had more to do; and so anxious was she, for his sake
and her own, to do it well, that she forced herself, after a
moment's recollection, to welcome him, with a look and manner
that were almost easy, and almost open; another struggle,
another effort still improved them . . .
Her manners gave some re-assurance to Edward, and he had
courage enough to sit down.   (241)

Her efforts, however, go for nothing once Marianne makes her
entrance. Instead of paying equal attention to all the guests,
Marianne indulges herself in exclamations of affection for Edward
and hints to Lucy that she should leave. Her intention is to express
'love and esteem' for Edward and Elinor, and to provide them with
a chance to be alone together. Lucy's feelings are of no interest to
her. However, given the real nature of the relationships between
Edward, Lucy and Elinor, all Marianne actually manages to do is to
distress the objects of her affection:

'What! are you never to hear yourself praised!—Then, you must
be no friend of mine; for those who will accept of my love and
esteem, must submit to my open commendation!'
The nature of her commendation, in the present case, however,
happened to be particularly ill-suited to the feelings of two thirds
of her auditors, and was so very unexhilarating to Edward, that
he very soon got up to go away.   (244)

Marianne's failure to meet the needs of those she loves results not
so much from the mere fact of her outspokenness as from its
spontaneity. Were her expressions of feeling based on observation of
the situation, mood and behaviour of the person at whom they are
directed, they might have some chance of accomplishing their
purpose. This failure of observation, however, is not accidental;
Marianne places great faith in her subjective responses, regardless of
the poverty of evidence on which they might be founded. Like the
romantic heroine whom Jane Austen mocks in *Northanger Abbey*,
Marianne is not far from believing that she 'could learn or
understand any thing before she was taught' (14). When questioned
by Elinor about the propriety of visiting Allenham in Mrs Smith's
absence, for example, Marianne argues that her feelings would have
revealed anything improper: 'if there had been any real impropriety
in what I did, I should have been sensible of it at the time, for we

always know when we are acting wrong' (68). Impartial consideration of circumstances is thus irrelevant to her. Ultimately,
however, this attitude does far more harm to Marianne herself than
to any of those who have to suffer her blundering displays of
affection. Given her philosophical assumptions, Marianne will not
accept Elinor's contention that even the most mediocre of formal
social activity is worthy of attention because of the opportunities it
provides for making judgements. Therefore, she frequently either
withdraws completely from involvement with others or, if unable to
do this, ignores what is going on around her. As a result, she deprives
herself of a number of opportunities to gain a better understanding
of her world.

There are two incidents in particular which demonstrate the
advantages of remaining within the formal context. The first is the
evening party given by Mrs Jennings. Deliberate secrecy and lack of
interest in conversation ensure that only the very alert individual
can gather information from most of the formal gatherings in *Sense
and Sensibility*. The party at Mrs Jennings' house in Berkeley Street,
however, is an exception. There is far more talk than usual, and, for
anyone willing to pay attention, there is the reward of several hard
facts and a number of significant hints. The revelation of
Willoughby's engagement to the wealthy Miss Grey provides some
explanation of his change in attitude to Marianne. Mrs Jennings'
repeated acts of kindness to Marianne, and her evident distaste for
Willoughby's materialism, reveal her as a much more substantial
person than could ever have been suspected from her behaviour at
Barton. And Colonel Brandon's moral stature is enhanced by Mrs
Jennings' description of Delaford as 'a nice old fashioned
place . . . close to the church' (196–7), and by his own unselfish
reaction to the news of Willoughby's engagement:

> Mrs Jennings, who had watched them with pleasure while they
> were talking, and who expected to see the effect of Miss
> Dashwood's communication, in such an instantaneous gaiety on
> Colonel Brandon's side, as might have become a man in the
> bloom of youth, of hope and happiness, saw him, with amaze-
> ment, remain the whole evening more serious and thoughtful
> than usual.   (200)

Marianne, however, misses all of this. Because her grief at the loss of
Willoughby is so great, and her concern for the group so minimal,

she soon withdraws to the privacy of her room. Even during the brief period that she is present, however, 'the abstraction of her thoughts preserved her in ignorance of every thing that was passing before her' (193). Elinor, on the other hand, refuses to allow personal feelings to take precedence over her social responsibilities. Although she is upset by her recent discovery of Edward's engagement, she stays for the whole evening, and, by paying attention to everything that goes on around her, gains significant insights into the moral shape of her world.

The only occasions on which Marianne is at all interested in social involvement are those on which her beloved Willoughby is present, and then she has 'no eyes for any one else' (53).[8] Participation of this kind does nothing, of course, to alleviate Marianne's general lack of awareness about her world, but we might expect that it would at least give her a thorough knowledge of Willoughby. This does not turn out to be the case, however, because she is so much under the direction of her illusions and her emotions that she never pays much attention to how Willoughby actually conducts himself. After she is snubbed by him at the London ball, for example, Marianne immediately gives in to her feelings, weeps piteously, and demands to be taken home. Consequently, she fails to observe anything of Willoughby's behaviour beyond the bare fact that he has rejected her. This leaves Marianne in such ignorance of what has really happened that, albeit only for a moment, she is able to convince herself that Willoughby is not the agent of her unhappiness:

'Elinor, I have been cruelly used; but not by Willoughby.'

'Dearest Marianne, who but himself? By whom can he have been instigated?'

'By all the world, rather than by his own heart . . . Beyond you three, is there a creature in the world whom I would not rather suspect of evil than Willoughby, whose heart I know so well?'   (189)

For all her knowledge of Willoughby's heart, Marianne proves to be a poorer judge of his character even than Sir John Middleton, who comes somewhat closer to the mark when he declares him 'a scoundrel of a fellow! such a deceitful dog!' (215). It is, however, by contrast to Elinor that Marianne's inadequacies are most sharply revealed. Although she is very much occupied with comforting her sister and with encouraging her to compose herself, Elinor notices everything that goes on. As a result she is able to achieve a complete view of Willoughby. His performance is disgraceful, but it is invested with a sense of shame that convinces Elinor that he is not utterly immoral:

> Her indignation would have been still stronger than it was, had she not witnessed that embarrassment which seemed to speak a consciousness of his own misconduct, and prevented her from believing him so unprincipled as to have been sporting with the affections of her sister from the first, without any design that would bear investigation. (178–9)

Events prove the wisdom of Elinor's assessment. Thus, even though she claims to be 'much better acquainted with him, than . . . with any other creature in the world' (59), it turns out that Marianne does not understand even Willoughby as well as Elinor.

The second pattern that I would like to consider also emphasises the need to make judgements. In the course of *Sense and Sensibility*, visits take Elinor and Marianne Dashwood into four distinct social milieus. These are Sir John Middleton's estate at Barton, Mrs Jennings' house in Berkeley Street, the fashionable London houses of the social circle that gathers around Mrs Ferrars and the John Dashwoods, and Cleveland, the home of Mr Palmer. None of them provides a model of excellence, and Marianne Dashwood has equal contempt for each. There are, however, as Elinor realises, crucial differences between them. Affairs are conducted in Berkeley Street and at Cleveland, for example, in such a way as to reveal a sense of social obligations that is completely missing at Barton. This does not, however, leave Barton at the bottom of the novel's moral hierarchy. The Middletons' aimless sociability has little value, but neither does it do much harm. The Ferrars–Dashwood group, on the other hand, is so obsessed with prestige and wealth that it poses a direct threat to the established order of things. An examination of the kind of formal social occasions that take place in each location reveals the precise nature of these differences.

The great limitation of life at Barton Park, the first of the moral universes with which we become acquainted, is that neither Sir John nor Lady Middleton has any conception of the proper function of the social ritual. Both are eager for company, but this is simply because they lack inner resources—Sir John is amazed that the Dashwood sisters can find so much with which to occupy themselves (40)—and they are happy only when Sir John can display his hospitality and Lady Middleton her elegance:

> They were scarcely ever without some friends staying with them in the house, and they kept more company of every kind than any other family in the neighbourhood. It was necessary to the happiness of both; for however dissimilar in temper and outward behaviour, they strongly resembled each other in that total want of talent and taste which confined their employments, unconnected with such as society produced, within a very narrow compass . . . Continual engagements at home and abroad, however, supplied all the deficiencies of nature and education; supported the good spirits of Sir John, and gave exercise to the good-breeding of his wife.   (32)

Since their very being is bound up in having company, they define the success of any gathering entirely by its size. Thus, on an evening when Mrs Jennings embarrasses both Dashwood sisters with her teasing, when Lady Middleton's children are allowed to become the centre of attention, and when Marianne's piano-playing is rudely interrupted, Sir John finds only the smallness of the group worthy of apology (33).

Those things which should be of real concern to a host are granted no importance by the Middletons. Rational conversation, for example, is replaced at Barton by gossip, game playing and noisy children, who 'put an end to every kind of discourse except what related to themselves' (34). On one occasion Elinor chides herself for being so naïve as to believe that an evening party at Barton might provide her with a chance to talk to Lucy Steele: 'The card-table was then placed, and Elinor began to wonder at herself for having ever entertained a hope of finding time for conversation at the park' (144).

Neither do the Middletons pay any heed to their own manners or to those of their guests. Sir John, in particular, sets a bad example. Thus, he talks while Marianne plays the piano, he divulges the private affairs of the Dashwood sisters to any casual visitor, and he introduces the Palmers by shouting in through the windows of Barton Cottage (105). Given the inadequacy of his own performance, it is hardly surprising that Sir John makes no attempt to check Mrs Jennings when she teases and torments Elinor and Marianne, or when she persists in questioning Colonel Brandon about the reasons for his sudden journey to London (63–4).

Furthermore, Sir John and Lady Middleton do not take advantage of the opportunities provided even by formal social gatherings as imperfect as theirs for observing the behaviour of others, and so for learning more about their relative moral worth. So far as they are concerned, all guests are company and, as such, equally valuable. The Steele sisters, for example, need display only a smartness of dress, civil manners and a concern for the furniture and the children, to win Lady Middleton's good opinion. Her praise is enough to inspire Sir John, who is already pleased to have discovered unexpected guests, into declaring them 'the sweetest girls in the world' (119).

The rude way in which Mrs Jennings and Mr Palmer behave during their visits to Barton suggests that there is little to choose between them and their hosts. Marianne is certainly of this opinion. However, final judgements of the kind Marianne makes should be deferred until they have been viewed within the context of their own homes, where they will be called upon to set the moral tone, rather than simply to follow the lead of another. And, indeed, the quality of social intercourse in Berkeley Street and at Cleveland turns out to be very different than at Barton. Certainly, there are aspects of life in Mrs Jennings' house that would not be unfamiliar to Sir John or Lady Middleton, because she continues to gossip and to intrude. Nevertheless, there is a crucial difference, as is revealed by Mrs Jennings' dinner party, the essential point of which is not to provide the host with entertainment, but to meet the needs of the guests. Thus, although her efforts are often comically inadequate, Mrs Jennings wins our admiration for the good hearted way in which she tries to alleviate Marianne's suffering:

'Poor soul!' cried Mrs Jennings, as soon as she was gone, 'how it grieves me to see her! And I declare if she is not gone away without finishing her wine! And the dried cherries too! Lord! nothing seems to do her any good. I am sure if I knew of any thing she would like, I would send all over the town for it.'   (194)

A similar sense of obligation to others is evident later when Mrs Jennings offers Edward Ferrars a home. Sir John Middleton might well have been equally ready to receive Edward at Barton—after

all, he would be company—but it is unlikely that his action would
have been based upon an attention to what is 'fit' for the object of his
kindness:

'Poor young man!' cried Mrs Jennings, 'I am sure he should be
very welcome to bed and board at my house; and so I would tell
him if I could see him. It is not fit that he should be living about at
his own charge now, at lodgings and taverns.'   (268)

Cleveland is a location which promises good things:

Cleveland was a spacious, modern-built house, situated on a
sloping lawn. It had no park, but the pleasure-grounds were
tolerably extensive; and like every other place of the same degree
of importance, it had its open shrubbery, and closer wood walk, a
road of smooth gravel, winding round a plantation, led to the
front, the lawn was dotted over with timber, the house itself was
under the guardianship of the fir, the mountain-ash, and the
acacia, and a thick screen of them altogether, interspersed with
tall Lombardy poplars, shut out the offices.   (302)

And, as it turns out, Mr Palmer is quite capable of providing the
kind of protection and security that is suggested by the relationship
of house to trees. In his ritual performance as host, for example, he
consistently demonstrates an awareness of his responsibilities and is
always 'perfectly the gentleman in his behaviour to all his visitors'
(304). Mr Palmer's moral capacity, though, is revealed most
decisively by his reaction to Marianne's illness. Dangerous though
her infection is, he remains with her until forced away by an even
greater obligation to his wife and child, and thus displays 'real
humanity and good-nature' (308). By setting this kind of example,
Mr Palmer is able to exercise a moral influence on others, most
notably Mrs Jennings. At Barton, she proved herself quite capable
of sinking to the level of the Middletons, but Mr Palmer inspires her
to behave as she does in her own home. Thus, when her host leaves,
Mrs Jennings,

with a kindness of heart which made Elinor really love her,
declared her resolution of not stirring from Cleveland as long as
Marianne remained ill, and of endeavouring, by her own

attentive care, to supply to her the place of the mother she had
taken her from.   (308)

The novel's fourth location considerably extends the moral scope
of *Sense and Sensibility*. Barton, the worst of the three environments so
far considered, is a moral non-entity; but it is in no sense evil.
Indeed, it has an air of almost prelapsarian innocence about it,
which is reflected in Jane Austen's description of Barton Valley: 'a
view of Barton Valley as they entered it gave them cheerfulness. It
was a pleasant fertile spot, well wooded, and rich in pasture' (28).
Barton society, which is essentially non-moral, is, then, much to be
preferred to the actively immoral one which is centred on Park and
Harley Streets, and conducts its affairs in rooms 'splendidly lit up,
quite full of company, and insufferably hot' (175). The leaders of
this society are Mrs Ferrars, her son Robert and the John
Dashwoods, and they combine the worst of aristocratic snobbery
and bourgeois materialism. It is thus very apt that Elinor's first
London encounter with Robert Ferrars and John Dashwood should
be in Grays, the jewellers, since this is a place dedicated to the twin
motives of profit and self-aggrandisement, or, as Mrs Jennings
would put it, 'money and greatness' (259). The ability of both to
corrupt is made evident by the manners of the two men. Robert
Ferrars is so concerned with picking out a tooth-pick case fit for a
man, 'adorned in the first style of fashion' (221), that he is totally
unaware of the needs of others and keeps the Dashwood sisters
waiting for fifteen minutes:

> All that could be done was, to sit down at that end of the counter
> which seemed to promise the quickest succession; one gentleman
> only was standing there, and it is probable that Elinor was not
> without hopes of exciting his politeness to a quicker dispatch. But
> the correctness of his eye, and the delicacy of his taste, proved to
> be beyond his politeness.   (220)

John Dashwood is much less rude, but proves to be just as ignorant
of the purpose of good manners. So far as he is concerned, civility
should be doled out in proportion to the wealth of the person
receiving it. Marianne and Elinor may be his sisters, but they are
not rich, and so, as he freely admits, were not considered worthy of
an early visit:

'I wished very much to call upon you yesterday,' said he, 'but it was impossible . . . *This* morning I had fully intended to call on you, if I could possibly find a spare half hour, but one has always so much to do on first coming to town . . . But to-morrow I think I shall certainly be able to call in Berkeley-street.'   (221–2)

Even this third day visit might not have been contemplated if it had not been for the possibility of meeting Mrs Jennings, 'a woman of very good fortune' (222). John Dashwood's actual response to Mrs Jennings, and to Colonel Brandon, whom he meets at her house, further illustrates his distorted concept of propriety:

His manners . . . to Mrs Jennings [were] most attentively civil; and on Colonel Brandon's coming in soon after himself, he eyed him with a curiosity which seemed to say, that he only wanted to know him to be rich, to be equally civil to *him*.   (223)

The vices of the Ferrars–Dashwood circle are accurately mirrored in the Harley Street dinner party, which deviates quite fundamentally from the proper purpose of the formal social gathering. John and Fanny Dashwood are completely unsuited to the roles of host and hostess because, for them, the point of the evening is not to find opportunities to meet the needs of the guests but to demonstrate their own importance: 'The dinner was a grand one, the servants were numerous, and every thing bespoke the Mistress's inclination for shew, and the Master's ability to support it' (233). As is the case at Barton, little value is placed on conversation: 'no poverty of any kind, except of conversation, appeared' (233). The best the ladies can manage when they retire to the drawing room, for example, is a discussion of the comparative heights of their children. In other respects, though, it is a much more unpleasant affair than even the most badly conducted of the Middletons' parties because, far from being ignored, manners become offensive weapons in a battle for power and prestige. Mrs Ferrars, for example, is consistently rude to Elinor in order to emphasise that she does not consider her wealthy enough or of sufficient social standing to qualify as a suitable match for her son, Edward. When Elinor enters the room Mrs Ferrars 'eyed [her] with the spirited determination of disliking her at all events' (232). Later in the evening her behaviour becomes even more directly aggressive, and she manipulates a conversation about painting so as to emphasise Elinor's social inferiority:

'Do you not think they [Elinor's screens] are something in Miss Morton's style of painting, ma'am?—*She does* paint most delightfully!—How beautifully her last landscape is done!'
'Beautifully indeed! But *she* does every thing well.'   (235)

The subject of Elinor's screens also gives John Dashwood the opportunity to make illegitimate use of polite behaviour. Dashwood is convinced that Colonel Brandon is interested in Elinor, and since he is concerned that she might eventually become a financial burden, he is determined to do all he can to improve her chances of a good marriage. Therefore, he displays the screens to Brandon as evidence that his prospective bride possesses the necessary accomplishments:

these screens, catching the eye of John Dashwood on his following the other gentlemen into the room, were officiously handed by him to Colonel Brandon for his admiration.
'These are done by my eldest sister,' said he; 'and you, as a man of taste, will, I dare say, be pleased with them.'   (234)

In a sense John Dashwood's polite gesture is aimed at serving Elinor. However, since it succeeds in reducing her to a commodity in the marriage market rather than elevating her as a human being, it completely misses the goal towards which good manners should be directed.

Through visits, then, Jane Austen creates four quite distinct and clearly defined worlds. By so doing, she introduces a curious kind of imbalance into the novel, because the reader ends up with a rather better sense of the minor characters than he does of Colonel Brandon or Edward Ferrars. There are, for example, two complete scenes—a morning visit to Barton Cottage and a dinner party at Barton Park (106–17)—devoted to the Palmers, whereas there is no one occasion when the novel's two most important male characters become the centre of attention. This is not to deny, however, the necessity of these visits because they facilitate the marking out of moral divisions. If they had not been introduced, and the large cast of characters with whom Elinor and Marianne come into contact had been allowed to blur together, then there would seem little point in Elinor's concern with observing and making judgements. Furthermore, by delineating her worlds so precisely, Jane Austen ensures that the reader can confirm for himself that the moral hierarchy created by Elinor's judgements is correct. As a result her stature is increased, particularly at the expense of Marianne, whose tendency to flatten out distinctions is made to look extremely foolish.

No amount of attention to the social rituals in *Sense and Sensibility* could bring Edward Ferrars into prominence because he is simply never given the chance to act in the polite context. However, Colonel Brandon can be made to stand out a little if attention is paid to a pattern of contrasts established between him and some of the other characters. Although it is rare for Brandon to assert himself during formal gatherings, when he does Jane Austen usually makes something out of it by emphasising the superiority of his behaviour to that of his companions. In this way she provides some foundation for his otherwise putative role as one of the novel's moral centres. There are three occasions, for instance, during social evenings at Barton Park on which Colonel Brandon shows himself to be a cut above his companions.

When Marianne plays the piano during one of the Middletons' parties, the response of her audience is generally unsatisfactory. Sir John is highly enthusiastic about her performance, but does not bother to listen; Lady Middleton makes protestations of interest, but cannot remember what has been played:

> Sir John was loud in his admiration at the end of every song, and as loud in his conversation with the others while every song lasted. Lady Middleton frequently called him to order, wondered how any one's attention could be diverted from music for a moment, and asked Marianne to sing a particular song which Marianne had just finished.   (35)

Colonel Brandon's reaction stands in sharp contrast: 'Colonel Brandon alone, of all the party, heard her without being in raptures. He paid her only the compliment of attention' (35).

Although Marianne is the victim in this instance, her social performance is in many ways no better than the Middletons', and on a later occasion she too proves to be inferior to Brandon. When Margaret embarrasses Elinor by feeding Mrs Jennings information about the identity of her lover, Marianne, in her customary way, leaps to her sister's defence. However, her angry attempts to silence Margaret serve only to incite her to give further clues:

> Marianne felt for her most sincerely; but she did more harm than good to the cause, by turning very red, and saying in an angry manner to Margaret,
> 'Remember that whatever your conjectures may be, you have no right to repeat them.'   (61)

Colonel Brandon's reaction to the situation is much more appropriate because, unlike Marianne, he keeps complete control over himself, and 'mindful [only] of the feelings of others' (62) diverts attention away from Elinor by engaging Lady Middleton in a conversation about the weather.

The moral differences between Colonel Brandon and Willoughby are established by a comparison of their respective behaviour in relation to the Whitwell excursion. When Colonel Brandon announces that he must leave at once for London, and so cancel the visit to Whitwell, he makes himself very unpopular with the others because they believe he is acting in an unnecessarily rigid way. Marianne sees no reason why the party should not proceed in his absence, and Willoughby suggests that the journey to London could be deferred. For them the enjoyment of the moment has large claims, and Brandon's failure to comply with their wishes marks him out as one of those people 'who cannot bear a party of pleasure' (65). Brandon, though, never hesitates in his decision because he respects the owner's wish that no one visit Whitwell unless accompanied by him, and because the needs of Miss Williams demand that he leave at once for London. Willoughby's subsequent behaviour runs in direct contradiction to Brandon's and thus reveals that he has none of his concern with propriety and sense of duty. First, in order to salvage some enjoyment from the day, Willoughby takes Marianne to his aunt's house at Allenham without the permission or the knowledge of the owner, and by so doing commits the very offence that Brandon has been so careful to avoid. Then, a few days later, Willoughby too announces that he must go to London, and like Brandon he will not say why. The similarity though is only superficial. Brandon gains no personal advantage from concealment, and is secretive only to protect Miss Williams' reputation. Willoughby, on the other hand, is leaving to find a more profitable match than Marianne, and so is secretive to protect himself.

Further contrasts are developed during the London and Cleveland sections of *Sense and Sensibility*, which demonstrate that, even at their best, Mrs Jennings and Sir John Middleton are not Brandon's equals. Mrs Jennings is by no means insensitive to Marianne Dashwood's grief over the loss of Willoughby, and Sir John is aware that she has been mistreated. Neither, however, seems to realise that the situation is also painful for Elinor, and they go to such excesses in making their feelings known to her that even Lady Middleton's complete lack of interest becomes welcome: 'The calm and polite unconcern of Lady Middleton on the occasion was an happy relief to Elinor's spirits, oppressed as they often were by the clamorous kindness of the others' (215). Colonel Brandon, by contrast, is able to combine concern with restraint, and is a real source of comfort to Elinor: 'Colonel Brandon's delicate un-obtrusive inquires were never unwelcome to Miss Dashwood' (216).

Even at Cleveland, where Mrs Jennings surpasses herself, she is unable to match Colonel Brandon. Her efforts to help Marianne are irreproachable, but she lacks sufficient control of her feelings to be of much use to Elinor: 'her conviction of her sister's danger would not allow her to offer the comfort of hope' (313). Colonel Brandon, however, although probably even more concerned about Marianne, never loses sight of Elinor's needs. When a messenger is required to bring Mrs Dashwood to Marianne's bedside, he offers his services in a way that combines calmness and urgency of purpose in just the right proportions to set Elinor's mind at rest:

> The comfort of such a friend at that moment as Colonel Brandon—of such a companion for her mother,—how gratefully was it felt!—a companion whose judgement would guide, whose attendance must relieve, and whose friendship might sooth her!—as far as the shock of such a summons *could* be lessened to her, his presence, his manners, his assistance, would lessen it.
>
> *He*, meanwhile, whatever he might feel, acted with all the firmness of a collected mind, made every necessary arrangement with the utmost dispatch, and calculated with exactness the time in which she might look for his return.   (311–12)

Colonel Brandon has little ritual communication with the Dashwood–Ferrars group, but he does on one occasion prove his superiority in a quite practical way. When Edward Ferrars' engagement to Lucy Steele becomes known, Mrs Ferrars, Robert, and the John Dashwoods react with a mixture of outrage and wonder. For Edward to have made such an unprofitable match is taken as a personal affront by Mrs Ferrars and Fanny Dashwood, and his mother's decision to disinherit him is regarded as perfectly justifiable. Only Robert Ferrars affects any concern for 'Poor Edward' (299), but he is soon satisfied by the thought that he has brought misfortune down on his own head. This then is what family feeling and loyalty amount to in a world given over to considerations of prestige and wealth. Colonel Brandon is barely acquainted with Edward Ferrars, and so there is no particular reason why he should be concerned with his affairs. Yet, because Elinor has given a good report of his character, and because he is in need, Brandon offers Edward the Barton living. Such a selfless gesture is beyond John Dashwood's comprehension, as must be Elinor's explanation of Brandon's behaviour: ' "It is truly astonishing!"—he cried, after hearing what she said—"what could be the Colonel's motive?"

"A very simple one—to be of use to Mr Ferrars." ' (295)

The ritual action of *Sense and Sensibility*, then, serves both to clarify Jane Austen's intentions and to reinforce her assertions. Elinor's approach to experience is vindicated and her good judgement confirmed; Marianne's deficiencies are thoroughly exposed; and Colonel Brandon's worth is partially demonstrated. Nevertheless, the problems outlined at the beginning of the chapter remain. The male characters, particularly Edward Ferrars, are not adequately realised; very little sense is given of Elinor's relationship with Edward or of Marianne's with Brandon; and none of the major characters demonstrates a sufficient grasp of the positive function of manners. As a result the Barton–Delaford community is unable to support the weight of moral authority which is finally placed upon it. My approach to *Sense and Sensibility* doubtless brings its limitations into greater prominence than might have been the case had attention been focused on other important aspects of the novel, such as Elinor's consciousness. However, there is no escaping the fact that it suffers from a real failure to dramatise, and thus helps to demonstrate how much the success of Jane Austen's other novels depends on her ability to realise so much of her action through the interplay between characters, particularly lovers, within the context of the formal social occasion.

3 Pride and Prejudice

Courtship is relegated to the periphery of *Sense and Sensibility*, but it re-assumes a very central position in *Pride and Prejudice*. The subject is introduced by the novel's famous opening sentence: 'It is a truth universally acknowledged, that a single man in possession of a good fortune, must be in want of a wife' (3). And it remains in the forefront throughout the first chapter which is given over entirely to Mrs Bennet, 'the business of [whose] life was to get her daughters married' (5). The novel's major plot threads are set in motion by the arrival of four strangers in the village of Meryton, and the fabric is not completed until each is married—Darcy to Elizabeth Bennet, Bingley to Jane Bennet, Wickham to Lydia Bennet and Mr Collins to Charlotte Lucas.[1] The choosing of partners is not simple, however, and seven unsuccessful courtships litter the path to the altar. Mr Collins is rejected by Elizabeth; Wickham tries to elope with Georgiana Darcy, pays attention to Miss King, and becomes briefly involved with Elizabeth; Elizabeth and Colonel Fitzwilliam are prevented from pursuing a mutual attraction by financial considerations; Darcy is involved with Caroline Bingley and, at least in Lady Catherine de Bourgh's mind, is the suitor of Anne de Bourgh. At the centre of this web of courtships is that of Darcy and Elizabeth, for it is through the development of their relationship that the novel makes its main statement. The other love affairs are subordinate and their function is largely exhausted once they have fulfilled the role of expanding or modifying the issues raised between hero and heroine.

In Jane Austen's novels difficulties between hero and heroine are usually created, and their final union delayed, by the immaturity that one or both of them brings into their relationship. In *Northanger Abbey*, *Sense and Sensibility* and *Emma*, the heroines are deficient; Catherine Morland lacks discrimination, Marianne Dashwood has an inflated sense of her innate abilities, and Emma is an 'imaginist' (335). In *Persuasion*, on the other hand, it is the faults of the hero that cause problems because Wentworth allows his judgement to be

64

clouded by feelings of resentment. And in *Mansfield Park*, both Fanny Price and Edmund Bertram are inadequate, she being too reticent and he too easily taken in by charm. *Pride and Prejudice*, however, does not obviously conform to this pattern, in that both Darcy and Elizabeth Bennet are extremely mature people by the time that they meet.[2] The mediocrity of her environment has made Elizabeth think too well of her admittedly excellent intelligence, but otherwise she has few personal flaws and many virtues. Amongst the most notable of these is the 'quickness of observation' (15) which enables her to see through the Bingley sisters' charming façade. They possess 'the power of being agreeable,' but Elizabeth almost immediately recognises that they are 'proud and conceited' (15). Elizabeth is also morally sound. This is particularly evident in her thoughts about marriage, which are characterised by a concern with establishing a proper relationship between the demands of personal feeling and the need for financial security. And furthermore, Elizabeth can mount a social performance that is brilliant and daring but always proper. Her arrival at Netherfield, for example, flushed and muddy after a three-mile walk across the fields, is unorthodox, but is perfectly appropriate to the needs of the situation created by her sister's illness. Darcy, too, has many good qualities. As master of Pemberley, he acts in accordance with the highest moral standards; his intelligence is sharp enough to cut straight through Bingley's vague logic (48–9); his manners are dignified if rather too reserved; and he possesses excellent judgement—Caroline Bingley's elegant posturings, for instance, come no closer to deceiving Darcy than they do Elizabeth Bennet.

Yet if we knew Darcy and Elizabeth only through their encounters with each other, we would never suspect that they were so mature. Elizabeth completely and wilfully misjudges Darcy's character, overlooks Wickham's faults simply because he is Darcy's enemy, and behaves towards Darcy with something approaching real insolence. Darcy is no better. At the Meryton ball he rudely rejects Bingley's proposal that he dance with Elizabeth. Later, he treats Mrs Bennet with obvious scorn, joins in the Bingley sisters' cruel gossip about the Bennet family, and finally proposes to Elizabeth in a way that suggests he feels almost as much loathing as love. This uncharacteristic immaturity can be explained by the fact that, although each is fairly knowing in the ways of his own social circle, neither has an accurate sense of the other's. Elizabeth Bennet is firmly located in a world of lesser gentry and bourgeoisie. Her father owns a small estate worth £2000 per annum, her mother is the daughter of an attorney, and her uncle, Mr Gardiner, is in trade. Darcy, on the other hand, belongs to the noble de Bourgh family, possesses the Pemberley estate, and has an income of £10,000 per annum, enough to put his among the four hundred most important families.[3] Lacking any experience of the other's world, each relies on stereotypes; Elizabeth accepts the common view that aristocrats are worthless snobs, and Darcy believes that anyone connected with trade must be vulgar and unworthy of respect. Unfortunately, since Darcy's visit to Meryton beings him into contact with Mrs Bennet, and since Elizabeth witnesses Darcy's supercilious behaviour at the Meryton ball, their first exposure to each other's worlds serves to confirm rather than disprove these stereotypes.

Further acquaintance gives Darcy and Elizabeth opportunities to refine their crude social typecasting. And Darcy does indeed quickly come to see some of Elizabeth's virtues. However, instead of re-examining her milieu in the light of the fact that it has produced at least one admirable person, he simply tries to isolate Elizabeth from her background. In his dealings with Elizabeth, Darcy begins to behave politely, but he continues to express contempt for the Bennet family and the people of Meryton. By so doing, Darcy provides Elizabeth with plenty of evidence to confirm her prejudices. However, the way in which Elizabeth reacts to Darcy suggests that her feelings towards him have their origins in more than simple moral disapproval. Even at his worst Darcy is no more objectionable than Lady Catherine de Bourgh or Mr Collins, and he is certainly not as bad as Wickham is finally revealed to be. Yet, for all her awareness of the faults of these people, Elizabeth is never rude to them. When it is necessary to let Wickham know that she has discovered the reality of his relationship with the Darcy family, Elizabeth does so with kindness and tact, and ends on a placatory note: 'Come, Mr Wickham, we are brother and sister, you know. Do not let us quarrel about the past. In future, I hope we shall be always of one mind' (329). Darcy's attempts to engage Elizabeth in conversations or dance, on the other hand, are greeted with ever more rude rebuffs. This kind of behaviour is so uncharacteristic of Elizabeth that we must assume that it has deep emotional roots. And, indeed, it seems likely that it derives from an unconscious need to deny that, for all his faults, she finds Darcy attractive. Up to this point in her life Elizabeth's emotional equilibrium has never been seriously challenged. Throughout her relationship with Wickham, for example, she is always extremely aware of how she feels, and can even discuss his defection to Miss King in a calm and analytical way: 'I am now convinced, my dear aunt, that I have never been much in love; for had I really experienced that pure and elevating passion, I should at present detest his very name, and wish him all manner of evil' (150). Therefore, it is not at all surprising that she should meet the threat Darcy poses by making every effort to drive him away, even though to do this she must repeatedly transgress the bounds of politeness.

Darcy is not put off by Elizabeth's rudeness, and in fact seems to sense the emotions that lie beneath it. As he explains later, her behaviour was such as to make him anticipate the success of his first marriage proposal, and Elizabeth acknowledges the ambiguity of her response to him:

'I believed you to be wishing, expecting my addresses.'
'My manners must have been in fault, but not intentionally I assure you.'   (369)

Therefore, in spite of his reservations about her background, Darcy makes many attempts to approach Elizabeth. Each time, Elizabeth rejects him. This creates an extremely frustrating situation and it is one that cannot be resolved until each has come to a better understanding of the other's social group. For all the attentions he pays her, Darcy will be unacceptable to Elizabeth so long as he fails to recognise that the gentry-middle class as a whole is worthy of his respect. And Elizabeth will continue to blind herself to Darcy's virtues until she has arrived at a fair estimation of the environment which has shaped him. Darcy's meeting with the excellent Gardiners, whose gentility is not diminished by the fact that they live within sight of their warehouses, and Elizabeth's introduction to Pemberley, a place that epitomises the taste, importance and enormous social responsibilities of the nobility, are necessary prerequisites of personal reconciliation.

The social and the personal are so closely bound together in the relationship between Elizabeth and Darcy that the larger implications of the marriage into which they finally enter are very evident. In her other novels Jane Austen tends to suggest that the continued moral well-being of society depends on the ability of the gentry to ward off the disruptive influence of the middle class and the aristocracy. But *Pride and Prejudice* concludes with a union which grows directly out of the ability of the participants to recognise that, in spite of their different functions, the middle class, the gentry and the nobility are all committed to the ideal of concern for others. The materialism and vulgarity of the bourgeoisie are as much in evidence in *Pride and Prejudice* as they were in *Northanger Abbey* and *Sense and Sensibility*. So is the snobbery of the aristocracy. But here people like Charlotte Lucas and Lady Catherine de Bourgh represent deviations from the norm of their groups rather than the norm itself.

Since courtship contributes so much to the themes of *Pride and Prejudice*, it is appropriate that dancing, which is, as Henry Tilney points out, the courtship ritual *par excellence*, should play a major part in its structure. Four incidents involving invitations to dance lay the groundwork for a pattern of approach and rejection which serves as an emblem of Darcy's relationship with Elizabeth. Other dance invitations—Bingley's to Jane, Collins' to Elizabeth and Wickham's to Elizabeth—provide a commentary on the problems and misunderstandings that exist between Darcy and Elizabeth. The dance disappears from the novel after the Netherfield ball, and emphasis is transferred to the visit. By comparing her impressions of Rosings and Pemberley Elizabeth is finally able to achieve a proper understanding of the aristocracy. Darcy's perspective on the middle class is similarly broadened by his meetings with Mr Collins and Sir William Lucas at Rosings, and the Gardiners at Pemberley. Consequently the pattern of approach and rejection which was continued at Rosings is broken at Pemberley when Elizabeth accepts several invitations in rapid succession. These temporary polite unions promise something more permanent, and the final section of *Pride and Prejudice* is organised around three marriages, those between Lydia and Wickham, and Bingley and Jane, quite literally clearing the way for Darcy and Elizabeth's.

Pride and Prejudice is much cleaner in its structural lines than either *Northanger Abbey* or *Sense and Sensibility*. In both of these novels patterns have to be extricated from an often confusing plethora of formal social occasions, and in *Sense and Sensibility* come nowhere near to providing an adequate vehicle for all its themes. *Pride and Prejudice*, on the other hand, readily divides into three sections, each controlled by a different and thematically appropriate social ritual—dancing for the problems of courtship, the visit for the broadening of social horizons, and marriage for the resolution of conflicts. It is not in its patterning alone, however, that *Pride and*

Prejudice reveals Jane Austen's increasing sense of the possibilities of the formal social occasion. The Netherfield ball scene surpasses anything to be found in the earlier novels because it not only plays its part in the dance invitation motif, but also serves as a microcosm of the relationships and issues developed in the first section of the novel. This use of the extended scene prefigures the complex individual formal social occasions we find in *Mansfield Park* and *Emma*, such as the Sotherton excursion, the theatricals, the Crown ball and the trip to Donwell.

The connection between marriage and dancing is rarely more obvious than in the early pages of *Pride and Prejudice*, for the arrival of a new tenant at Netherfield causes Mrs Bennet and her younger daughters to talk of little else. Partners for the evening and partners for life become almost indistinguishable as Mrs Bennet's mind rushes on anxiously towards matrimony:

> To be fond of dancing was a certain step towards falling in love; and very lively hopes of Mr Bingley's heart were entertained.
> 'If I can but see one of my daughters happily settled at Netherfield,' said Mrs Bennet to her husband, 'and all the others equally well married, I shall have nothing to wish for.'   (9)

Outside of Mrs Bennet's imagination, however, unions are not formed so easily, and Elizabeth Bennet and Darcy show little sign of becoming infected with the mating spirit. Far from considering marriage, Darcy neglects even to ask Elizabeth to dance at the Meryton Assembly, and manages to do so in a way that arouses her hostility. Because he regards Meryton society as vulgar, Darcy refuses to recognise that it can claim even the minimum of good manners from him. When Mrs Long, who 'does not keep a carriage, and had come to the ball in a hack chaise' (19) sits next to him, Darcy maintains an offensive silence for a full thirty minutes. It is not surprising, then, that he bridles at the sociable Bingley's attempts to make him join in the dancing:

> 'Which do you mean?' and turning round, he looked for a moment at Elizabeth, till catching her eye, he withdrew his own and coldly said, 'She is tolerable; but not handsome enough to tempt *me*; and I am in no humour at present to give consequence to young ladies who are slighted by other men.'   (11–12)

Further acquaintance with Elizabeth, however, soon modifies Darcy's attitude. Unattractive as he might find Meryton society in general, Darcy cannot long ignore the fact that Elizabeth is at least physically appealing: 'But no sooner had he made it clear to himself and his friends that she had hardly a good feature in her face, than he began to find it was rendered uncommonly intelligent by the beautiful expression of her dark eyes' (23). And at Sir William Lucas' party he discovers that she has more substantial virtues. The repartee in which Elizabeth engages him for eavesdropping on her conversation with Charlotte Lucas is charming, and her performance at the piano is admirable. Unlike her sister Mary, who has no sense of the limitations of her accomplishments, Elizabeth is aware that though her playing and singing are 'pleasing' they are 'by no means capital' (25). Consequently, to avoid taxing the interest of her audience, she tactfully gives up her place at the piano after a song or two. Darcy is so impressed by this display of concern for others that he begins to discriminate between Elizabeth and her world. The party as a whole clearly disgusts him, and when the guests begin to dance he expresses 'silent indignation at such a mode of passing the evening, to the exclusion of all conversation' (25). Sir William Lucas' ill-timed praise of dancing persuades Darcy to give voice to his feelings:

'There is nothing like dancing after all.—I consider it as one of the first refinements of polished societies.'
'Certainly, Sir;—and it has the advantage also of being in vogue amongst the less polished societies of the world.—Every savage can dance.'   (25)

Primitive and crude as the proceedings in general may appear to Darcy's prejudiced eyes, nevertheless he has no objection to joining in when Elizabeth Bennet is offered as a partner: ' "You cannot refuse to dance, I am sure, when so much beauty is before you." And taking her hand, he would have given it to Mr Darcy, who, though extremely surprised, was not unwilling to receive it' (26).

Because Darcy's attitude to her society is no better than it was when he rejected Bingley's similar proposal at the Meryton ball, Elizabeth is quite justified in refusing him. However, there seems to be more to her refusal than disapproval of his behaviour in two specific situations. After the Meryton ball, Elizabeth assured her mother that she would 'never . . . dance with him' (20). This suggests that she believes she knows the man in a very final sort of way, and that the arrogance she has observed constitutes the sum total of his character. That any part of Darcy's attitude to Meryton society might be justified, or that he might have other better qualities, completely escapes her. The source of Elizabeth's confidence in her understanding of Darcy's character is made very clear by a conversation with Charlotte Lucas. Elizabeth and Charlotte have very different attitudes to Darcy's pride. However, neither sees any reason to go beyond it for an explanation of his character because each regards this quality as the essential mark of the aristocrat. Thus Charlotte argues:

> His pride . . . does not offend *me* so much as pride often does, because there is an excuse for it. One cannot wonder that so very fine a young man, with family, fortune, every thing in his favour, should think highly of himself. If I may so express it, he has a *right* to be proud.   (20)

Elizabeth, on the other hand, takes the view that because of his pride, the aristocrat is inevitably offensive in his dealings with those he considers to be his inferiors: 'I could easily forgive *his* pride, if he had not mortified *mine*' (20). The Darcys created by Charlotte and Elizabeth bear more resemblance to the actual man than young Lucas' Squire–Westernish aristocrat, who 'keep[s] a pack of foxhounds, and drink[s] a bottle of wine every day' (20). Nevertheless, all three are essentially stereotypes, based on preconceived notions rather than on any observation of actual conduct, and as such are static figures incapable of moral growth. It is only because she views Darcy in such simplistic terms that Elizabeth can be so confident that she has complete knowledge of his character.

Elizabeth and Darcy have quickly developed an extremely frustrating relationship. He is attracted to her, but because he fails to go beyond stereotypes in approaching her milieu, and because of a combination of genuine objections to his behaviour and a similar weakness in her attitude to the aristocracy, there seems little chance that she will accept his advances. To emphasise the impasse at which Darcy and Elizabeth have arrived, Jane Austen introduces the approach and rejection movement, established by Darcy's unsuccessful dance invitation, into each of their four main formal encounters at Netherfield. The pattern is set by the events of the first evening. When Darcy tries to pay a compliment to Elizabeth,

whom Miss Bingley has just described as 'a great reader' (37), by
stating a preference for a woman who adds to all the usual skills and
talents 'something more substantial, in the improvement of her
mind by extensive reading' (39), she ignores the personal implications of his comments, and engages him in a sharp exchange
about feminine accomplishments:

'I am no longer surprised at your knowing *only* six accomplished
women. I rather wonder now at your knowing *any*.'
   'Are you so severe upon your own sex, as to doubt the
possibility of all this? '
   '*I* never saw such a woman. *I* never saw such capacity, and
taste, and application, and elegance, as you describe,
united.'   (39–40)

In that Darcy's attitude to her family and its middle-class
associations has still not improved, Elizabeth is justified in rejecting
his approach once again. It would, after all, be hard to expect her to
be receptive to a man who just previously had commented that the
possession of relatives in Cheapside 'must very materially lessen
their [Jane and Elizabeth's] chance of marrying men of any
consideration in the world', especially as his words contrast so
unfavourably with Bingley's generous comment that 'if they had
uncles enough to fill *all* Cheapside . . . it would not make them one
jot less agreeable' (37). Nevertheless, the way in which Elizabeth
deals with Darcy is far from satisfactory, because it shows that she
too is in the grip of obscuring prejudices. Darcy's comments on
accomplishments are serious and intelligent. Elizabeth, however, is
so obsessed with her stereotype that she simply twists his words and,
by denying that women exist who can match up to his ideal, suggests
that he is a snob who speaks only to assert his own superiority.
Consequently, she misses an opportunity to learn that there is
something more to Darcy than was apparent at the Meryton
Assembly. Elizabeth's failure to acknowledge Darcy's virtues is all
the more inexcusable because earlier in the evening she was given
information about his background that should have enabled her to
put his demands for intellectual seriousness in their proper context.
During a discussion about libraries, it becomes evident that
Pemberley is a place with a long tradition of respect for things of the
mind, and that Darcy is striving to maintain that tradition:

'What a delightful library you have at Pemberley, Mr Darcy!'
'It ought to be good,' he replied, 'it has been the work of many
generations.'
'And then you have added so much to it yourself, you are
always buying books.'
'I cannot comprehend the neglect of a family library in such
days as these.' (38)

Justifiable disapproval and prejudice alone, however, do not
provide a sufficient explanation for the particularly virulent style in
which Elizabeth rebuffs Darcy. She had just as much reason to think
badly of him at Sir William Lucas' party, and yet she turned him
down politely on that occasion: 'Indeed, Sir, I have not the least
intention of dancing.—I entreat you not to suppose that I moved
this way in order to beg for a partner' (26). Moreover, Elizabeth is
never overtly rude to Lady Catherine de Bourgh, although she fits
the aristocratic stereotype much better than Darcy and offers
considerable provocation. Even the most outrageous of Lady
Catherine's comments evoke nothing more than an amused or
ironic response from Elizabeth. Neither politeness nor detachment,
however, are characteristics of this Netherfield encounter with
Darcy. Instead Elizabeth seems to be in the grip of strong feelings.
Since the intention of Elizabeth's words is to hurt, hatred would
seem to be the most likely source of her passion. However, their
effect suggests something else. Instead of being offended by
Elizabeth's outburst, Darcy finds it attractive. Thus when Caroline
Bingley tries to take advantage of what seems a good opportunity to
discredit Elizabeth, she is surprised to find her malicious comments
turned against herself:

'Eliza Bennet,' said Miss Bingley, when the door was closed on
her, 'is one of those young ladies who seek to recommend
themselves to the other sex, by undervaluing their own; and with
many men, I dare say, it succeeds. But, in my opinion, it is a
paltry device, a very mean art.'
'Undoubtedly,' replied Darcy, to whom this remark was
chiefly addressed, 'there is meanness in *all* the arts which ladies
sometimes condescend to employ for captivation. Whatever
bears affinity to cunning is despicable.' (40)

For Darcy to respond in a way that amounts to a statement of preference for Elizabeth over Caroline clearly suggests that he has seen beneath the surface of Elizabeth's words. There was indeed a good deal of 'mean art' in them, although its aim was the opposite of what Caroline supposes, but there was also something akin to real affection.

With the addition of this new element, the relationship between Darcy and Elizabeth becomes even more difficult, and a spiral effect is created. Evidence that Elizabeth loves him encourages Darcy to intensify his approaches. Because she is unable to deal with the feelings aroused by these approaches, Elizabeth rejects him with ever increased violence. However, the more passion Elizabeth puts into warding off Darcy, the more affection he perceives, and the greater become his efforts to establish contact with her. The spiral ascends through several turns on the second day of Elizabeth's visit to Netherfield. A conversation about Bingley's hasty style of letter-writing quickly intensifies into a more general debate about the value of precipitance. Darcy's contribution to the discussion is intended only to make a rather limited plea for the value of acting upon a consideration of circumstances and with an attention to propriety. Elizabeth, however, broadens and distorts his arguments so as to suggest that he is placing a sterile concern with form ahead of the claims of 'friendship and affection' (50). Again, then, she reacts to his conversational approach by rudely hinting that he is a snob. Darcy, though, perceives more than insults in her words, for he makes a much more direct approach later in the evening. Inspired by Miss Bingley's playing of 'a lively Scotch air . . . Mr Darcy, drawing near Elizabeth, said to her—

"Do not you feel a great inclination, Miss Bennet, to seize such an opportunity of dancing a reel?" ' (51–2). This invitation is presumably only a theoretical one. It is nevertheless genuine in spirit, and would not have been extended unless Darcy had been anticipating that Elizabeth would respond rather more favourably than she did at the Lucas' party. In actuality he receives his most explicit rejection so far. With extreme perversity Elizabeth chooses to interpret his proposal as a snobbish attempt to expose her bad taste, and so turns it down:

> You wanted me, I know, to say 'Yes,' that you might have the pleasure of despising my taste; but I always delight in overthrowing those kind of schemes, and cheating a person of their

premeditated contempt. I have therefore made up my mind to tell you, that I do not want to dance a reel at all—and now despise me if you dare.   (52)

Darcy's rude treatment of Mrs Bennet during her visit only a few hours earlier justifies Elizabeth's continued disapproval. However, it becomes increasingly evident in the course of the day that her definition of him as an utter snob is inadequate, and that by clinging to it so rigidly she is depriving herself of opportunities to achieve a richer understanding of his character. The impropriety of Mrs Bennet's behaviour, for example, is a source of great embarrassment to Elizabeth herself: 'Darcy only smiled; and the general pause which ensued made Elizabeth tremble lest her mother should be exposing herself again' (45). Yet, she will not allow the possibility that Darcy's rudeness may have been caused by disapproval of Mrs Bennet's actual conduct as well as by objections to her low origins. Similarly, during the evening, because of her single-minded approach to Darcy, Elizabeth blinds herself to the fact that he is a man who possesses both a serious intelligence and sufficient *joie de vivre* to cherish the idea of dancing a reel.

The spiral ascends still further on the next day. Far from being put off by the refusal of his dance invitation, Darcy finds such a mixture of 'sweetness and archness in her manner' that he becomes quite 'bewitched' (52). Consequently, he responds to an attempt by Miss Bingley and Mrs Hurst to exclude Elizabeth from a morning walk, by immediately inviting her to join in. Elizabeth, however, not only refuses, but does so in such a way as to group Darcy with the snobbish Bingley sisters: 'No, no; stay where you are.—You are charmingly group'd, and appear to uncommon advantage. The picturesque would be spoilt by admitting a fourth' (53). Elizabeth's self-deceit is blatant. Darcy had 'felt [his companions'] rudeness' (53) and had acted to correct it. Thus, rather than being the snob Elizabeth labels him, Darcy has shown himself to be a man capable of attending to the needs of others.

A similar sequence of events occurs in the evening. Caroline Bingley's efforts to attract Darcy's attention by parading up and down the room are unsuccessful until she persuades Elizabeth to join her: 'Elizabeth was surprised, but agreed to it immediately. Miss Bingley succeeded no less in the real object of her civility; Mr Darcy looked up' (56). Elizabeth's response to Darcy's display of interest is to indulge herself in an extended mockery of his character.

She dwells on his supposed intimacy with the vain Caroline Bingley, twits him for his lack of humour, suggests that he believes himself to be perfect, and concludes by again accusing him of 'vanity and pride' (57). As usual Elizabeth is so busy repelling Darcy that she ignores indications that there is more to his character than she supposes. Darcy meets her accusation that he is guilty of vanity and pride by drawing distinctions between the words: 'Yes, vanity is a weakness indeed. But pride—where there is a real superiority of mind, pride will be always under good regulation' (57). Although she has already learnt from Mary that 'a person may be proud without being vain' (20), Elizabeth chooses to believe that Darcy is simply splitting semantic hairs in order to justify his own behaviour, and 'turned away to hide a smile' (57). Yet Darcy has provided some very clear guidelines to his strengths and weaknesses. He is guilty of pride in the sense of vanity, but he also posesses that proper pride that derives from an awareness of the importance of his role in society.

Since such a firm pattern of approach and rejection has been established, it is extremely surprising that when Darcy next asks Elizabeth to dance, at the Netherfield ball, she accepts: 'she found herself suddenly addressed by Mr Darcy, who took her so much by surprise in his application for her hand, that, without knowing what she did, she accepted him' (90). The phrase 'without knowing what she did' tells us why. There are many things on Elizabeth's mind during the Netherfield ball, including disappointment at Wickham's unexpected absence, and a mixture of amusement and repugnance at the revelation of Mr Collins' matrimonial intentions. When Darcy comes upon her, then, her conscious thoughts are elsewhere, and her feelings for once get a chance to express themselves. This does not mean, though, that Elizabeth is any closer to acknowledging her emotions. The interval between Darcy's invitation and the beginning of the dance gives her time to collect herself, and as they move down the set she makes determined efforts to re-establish some distance. First of all, she ridicules the surface formalities of the dance in order to deny its significance as a courtship ritual, and thus to deprive Darcy's invitation of its significance: 'It is *your* turn to say something now, Mr Darcy.—I talked about the dance, and *you* ought to make some kind of remark on the size of the room, or the number of couples' (91). This is sheer perversity, because Elizabeth is usually well aware of the larger implications of dancing. Certainly, when Mr Collins engaged her for the first two dances, Elizabeth immediately realised that he was planning to make her his wife: 'It now first struck her, that *she* was selected from among her sisters as worthy of being the mistress of Hunsford Parsonage' (88). Her other tactics include comments on Darcy's 'unsocial, taciturn disposition' (91). However, it is by making repeated and unnecessary references to her knowledge of Darcy's supposed mistreatment of Wickham that Elizabeth most effectively expresses her hostility: 'He has been so unlucky as to lose *your* friendship . . . and in a manner which he is likely to suffer from all his life' (92). Temporary acceptance is thus successfully translated into a promise of permanent separation:

> 'But if I do not take your likeness now, I may never have another opportunity.'
> 'I would by no means suspend any pleasure of yours,' he coldly replied. She said no more, and they went down the other dance and parted in silence.   (94)

The Netherfield ball brings the first movement of *Pride and Prejudice* to an end, and Jane Austen constructs it in such a way that it sums up and comments on many of the elements in the complex of attraction and repulsion that comprises the relationship which has developed between Darcy and Elizabeth. The differences in Elizabeth's reactions to her three partners, actual and would-be, remind us, for example, that she is usually a good deal more mature than in her dealings with Darcy. Although the possibility of dancing with the attractive Wickham has filled Elizabeth's thoughts prior to the ball, she responds sensibly to the disappointing realisation that he is not present:

> But Elizabeth was not formed for ill-humour; and though every prospect of her own was destroyed for the evening, it could not dwell long on her spirits; and having told all her griefs to Charlotte Lucas . . . she was soon able to make a voluntary transition to the oddities of her cousin.   (90)

This epitomises the secure emotional balance that Elizabeth displays throughout her friendship with Wickham. Although she takes Wickham as 'her model of the amiable and pleasing' (152), Elizabeth does not build up their relationship into more than it is, or lose touch with the fact that her feelings for him are rather limited.

The role Elizabeth had hoped Wickham would play is usurped by Mr Collins who claims the first two dances. It is clear to Elizabeth that Collins intends dancing to prepare the way for a marriage proposal. Matrimony is not something Elizabeth can afford to take lightly, because failure to find a husband will leave her in a state of relative poverty. And Collins is, in fact, well enough situated in life to guarantee her future security. Elizabeth's response to Collins, however, proves that she is unwilling to put self-interest ahead of principles. For her, marriage without affection and respect constitutes a sacrifice of 'every better feeling to worldly advantage' (125), and since Collins' character is so accurately reflected in his performance on the dance floor, Elizabeth separates from him without the slightest wish of extending their relationship:

> Mr Collins, awkward and solemn, apologising instead of attending, and often moving wrong without being aware of it, gave her all the shame and misery which a disagreeable partner for a couple of dances can give. The moment of her release from him was exstacy.   (90)

While dancing with Darcy, Elizabeth, as we have already seen, shows none of this knowledge of her emotions or regard for principles, even though Darcy tries to remind her of the moral implications of the polite performance: 'Are you consulting your own feelings in the present case, or do you imagine that you are gratifying mine?' (91). Equally lacking is the good judgement with which she approaches Collins. Darcy's attempts to warn her that she is mistaken about his relationship with Wickham are supported by Jane, who has made enquiries of Bingley, and by Caroline Bingley. Yet Elizabeth finds reasons to doubt all three, and will not allow that there might be any validity in their combined claims. The 'wilful ignorance' (95) of which Elizabeth accuses Miss Bingley in this instance more accurately reflects her own refusal to see beyond a version of events that conforms with her personal prejudices.

A similar lack of good judgement is evident in Elizabeth's interpretation of Darcy's attitude to her family and relatives. The Bennets behave particularly badly during the Netherfield ball:

> To Elizabeth it appeared, that had her family made an agreement to expose themselves as much as they could during the

evening, it would have been impossible for them to play their parts with more spirit, or finer success.   (101–2)

Mr Collins pays Darcy sycophantic attention; Mrs Bennet rattles on loudly about Jane's chances of marrying Bingley, and sneers at Darcy; Mary bores the guests with her weak singing; and Mr Bennet silences her rudely. Elizabeth is acutely aware that none of this escapes Darcy's attention, and is not entirely unjustified in believing that he reacts to their foolishness in a cruel and snobbish way:

> That his two sisters and Mr Darcy, however, should have such an opportunity of ridiculing her relations was bad enough, and she could not determine whether the silent contempt of the gentleman, or the insolent smiles of the ladies, were more intolerable.   (102)

But there is more to his response than this. While listening to Mrs Bennet, 'the expression of his face changed gradually from indignant contempt to a composed and steady gravity' (100), and during Mary's pretentious performance he refuses to share in the Bingley sisters' 'derision', and instead 'continued . . . impenetrably grave' (100). Gravity is a term used in the eighteenth century to define emotions of the most serious and dignified kind. For Darcy to register such feelings thus provides clear evidence that his attitude to the Bennets is shaped not only by vanity but also by a keen sensitivity to the moral implications of their actual behaviour. Elizabeth's prejudice, however, is too strong to allow her to see what is revealed in Darcy's face, and it comes as a surprise to her when he later explains that:

> The situation of your mother's family, though objectionable, was nothing in comparison of that total want of propriety so frequently, so almost uniformly betrayed by herself, by your three younger sisters, and occasionally even by your father.   (198)

In the midst of all this confusion, discord and misunderstanding, Bingley and Jane alone achieve harmony. This is emphasised by the tableau in which the scene ends:

> They [Miss Bingley and Mrs Hurst] repulsed every attempt of Mrs Bennet at conversation, and by so doing, threw a languor

over the whole party, which was very little relieved by the long speeches of Mr Collins, who was complimenting Mr Bingley and his sisters on the elegance of their entertainment, and the hospitality and politeness which had marked their behaviour to their guests. Darcy said nothing at all. Mr Bennet, in equal silence, was enjoying the scene. Mr Bingley and Jane were standing together, a little detached from the rest, and talked only to each other. Elizabeth preserved as steady a silence as either Mrs Hurst or Miss Bingley.   (102-3)

One of the functions of the dance invitation motif has been to establish similar contrasts between Bingley's relationship with Jane and Darcy's with Elizabeth throughout the first part of the novel. While Darcy refuses to dance with Elizabeth at the Meryton Assembly, Bingley dances twice with Jane. From that point on their relationship is one of approach and acceptance in contrast to the approach and rejection pattern that characterises all meetings between Darcy and Elizabeth. Thus, at the very moment when Elizabeth is busily engaged in repudiating Darcy at the Netherfield ball, Bingley and Jane pass by 'dancing together' (93). The ease with which Bingley and Jane draw together, however, is not so much intended to offer a contrast to the difficulties which beset Darcy and Elizabeth as to make a comment on them. Darcy and Elizabeth are kept apart by the belief that a deep social rift lies between them. Bingley and Jane illustrate how mistaken they are. Although Bingley, who 'inherited property to the amount of nearly an hundred thousand pounds from his father' (15), is much wealthier than Jane, he does not regard himself as her social superior. His background is in trade, and he has not yet acquired the essential qualification of the gentleman—ownership of land. The Bennets, on the other hand, are a long-established family in possession of an estate, albeit entailed. There is, then, much to be gained on both sides from a match between a rising man of fortune and the daughter of a rather faded gentleman. Since Bingley and Jane are social equals, it is illogical that Darcy should be willing to associate with the Bingleys, but not with the Bennets. In the one case he quite properly balances off wealth and acquired gentility against low origins; in the other he perversely focuses almost entirely on the middle-class element introduced through marriage. This is perhaps because he finds it easier to accommodate himself to the faults of the Bingley family, which derive mainly from the aristocratic posturings of Caroline Bingley and Mrs Hurst, than to the unaccustomed vulgarity of some members of the Bennet family. Elizabeth is no less perverse since, in spite of his sisters' aristocratic leanings, she accepts Bingley into her social universe, and yet she places his friend Darcy beyond the pale.

Some education is needed in order that Darcy and Elizabeth might come to recognise society as a network of interconnections broad enough to embrace Darcys, Bingleys and Bennets, and thereby clear the way for personal reconciliation. This is provided by visits to the aristocratic worlds of Rosings and Pemberley. Life at Rosings under Lady Catherine de Bourgh confirms Elizabeth's stereotypes, but Pemberley calls them into question, and compels her to arrive at a more complex and favourable view of the aristocracy. Darcy's perspective is broadened in a similar way. The behaviour of Collins and the Lucases at Rosings displays the middle class at its worst; but the Gardiners, to whom Darcy is introduced at Pemberley, prove that trade and gentility are not incompatible. A change in the personal relationship follows almost automatically from these reversals in social attitudes, and by the end of the visit to Pemberley Elizabeth is more than ready to accept Darcy as her suitor.

To emphasise the reversals which are achieved by the progression from Rosings to Pemberley Jane Austen organises this section of her novel around a series of antitheses. There are three main elements in Elizabeth's introduction to each house—a eulogy by a retainer, a view of the house and its park, and a meeting with the owner—and it is in the contrasts between them that the essential qualities of Rosings and Pemberley, and hence of the aristocracy, are revealed to her. The contrasting ways in which Collins and the Lucases on the one hand and the Gardiners on the other respond to aristocratic environments is equally revealing of the middle class, and provides the basis of Darcy's education. The transformation which is wrought in Darcy's relationship with Elizabeth as a result of social enlightenment is echoed in the substitution of a pattern of approach and acceptance at Pemberley for the approach and rejection motif which continues to predominate at Rosings.

Our acquaintance with Rosings begins a long time before we are actually granted a view of the estate or its owner. Mr Collins' first letter to Mr Bennet is full of the subject and whenever he is present thereafter, we are sure to hear more about it. Of course, none of what Collins says can be taken at face value, because it functions entirely at the level of eulogy and, in that Rosings has become his *raison d'être*, it would be hard to imagine a less objective guide. Nevertheless, he turns out to be ideal because, simply by being the kind of man he is, he captures the very spirit of the place. Indeed, it could be argued with some justice that once we know Collins we know Rosings and Lady Catherine de Bourgh. By all professional standards, Collins is completely unsuited to the clerical position granted him by Lady Catherine. Despite his displays of piety, which include subjecting the Bennet girls to readings of Fordyce, there is little evidence that he is motivated by any considerations but of self. It might be expected that a clergyman influenced by Fordyce would object to card-playing, dancing and singing. Collins, however, does not allow such scruples to interfere with his own amusement:

> 'I am by no means of opinion, I assure you,' said he, 'that a ball of this kind, given by a young man of character, to respectable people, can have any evil tendency; and I am so far from objecting to dancing myself that I shall hope to be honoured with the hands of all my fair cousins in the course of the evening.'   (87)

Collins' outline of a clergyman's duties also places a suspiciously strong emphasis on things of advantage to himself:

> The rector of a parish has much to do.—In the first place, he must make such an agreement for tythes as may be beneficial to himself and not offensive to his patron. He must write his own sermons; and the time that remains will not be too much for his parish duties, and the care and improvement of his dwelling, which he cannot be excused from making as comfortable as possible.   (101)

As if to compensate for laxness about his own religious obligations, Collins is excessively strenuous in dealing with the failings of others, and shows little awareness of Christian charity. The advice he offers the Bennets about Lydia's elopement, for example, runs in direct contradiction to the parable of the prodigal son: 'Let me advise you then, my dear Sir, to console yourself as much as possible, to throw off your unworthy child from your affection for ever, and leave her to reap the fruits of her own heinous offence' (297). Since Collins lacks any of the proper qualifications to be vicar of Rosings, we must assume that Lady Catherine's decision to entrust him with the spiritual life of the community under her charge was based entirely on his ability to offer her unstinted approval: 'I need not say you will be delighted with her. She is all affability and condescension' (157). This tells us something very important about how affairs are conducted at Rosings. Unlike the responsible landowner, who believes that the possession of an estate confers on him an obligation to attend to the needs of his tenants and local community, Lady Catherine, it seems, is concerned only with the ways in which Rosings can increase her own prestige. A clergyman who flatters her and broadcasts her virtue to the world is therefore preferable to one who takes his profession seriously.

Mrs Reynolds, Darcy's housekeeper, who introduces Elizabeth and the Gardiners to Pemberley, offers an equally illuminating but contrasting insight into the operations of the aristocratic estate. The manner in which she praises her employer has something of the eulogy about it too, and, in answering Mr Gardiner's comment about the possibility of Darcy marrying, she undoubtedly exaggerates his virtues: 'Yes, Sir; but I do not know when *that* will be. I do not know who is good enough for him' (248). However, whereas sycophantic regard for rank inspires Collins' hyperboles about Lady Catherine, it is the genuine 'pride' and 'attachment' (248) of an 'intelligent servant' (250) that cause Mrs Reynolds to speak so well of Darcy. Her knowledge of Darcy, his family and his house is intimate. She can speak with authority not only about Darcy's excellent conduct as master of Pemberley, but also of his virtues as a four-year-old child; she was personally acquainted with old Mr Darcy and, through their portraits, knows of the family forbears; and she can give precise information about the functions and trappings of every room in the Pemberley house. The master-servant relationship thus revealed is the proper one. Darcy does not expect his employees to be grovelling subordinates, but regards them as sensible human beings whose respect must be earned. Neither does he see them simply as instruments of labour, but rather as rational human beings who must be included in the community of the big house and introduced to Pemberley values in order that they might play their part in preserving proper social standards.

The second element in Elizabeth's introduction to the aristocratic world is her first view of the two great houses. A distant prospect of Rosings suggests that it was built to sustain a worthwhile ideal: 'It was a handsome modern building, well situated on rising

ground' (156). However, as interpreted by Mr Collins, whose tone is
rapturous, and whose attention is fixed on the number and cost of
the windows, it comes to represent pretension and materialism:

> Every park has its beauty and its prospects; and Elizabeth saw
> much to be pleased with, though she could not be in such raptures
> as Mr Collins expected the scene to inspire, and was but slightly
> affected by his enumeration of the windows in front of the house,
> and his relations of what the glazing altogether had originally
> cost Sir Lewis De Bourgh.   (161)

The interior reveals a similar discrepancy between original intention and present function. The entrance hall is of 'fine proportion' (161), but the furniture substitutes 'splendour' for 'elegance' (246).

Pemberley is not marred by any such failed ideals. At first sight
the park and the house not only create an impression of great dignity
but also display that balance of Art and Nature which in the
eighteenth century indicated moral worth as well as aesthetic
value.[4]

> It was a large, handsome, stone building, standing well on rising
> ground, and backed by a ridge of high woody hills;—and in front,
> a stream of some natural importance was swelled into greater, but
> without any artificial appearance. Its banks were neither formal,
> nor falsely adorned. Elizabeth was delighted. She had never seen
> a place for which nature had done more, or where natural beauty
> had been so little counteracted by an awkward taste.   (245)

Even when viewed from different perspectives through the windows
of the house, the grounds retain their perfection:[5] 'As they passed
into other rooms, these objects were taking different positions; but
from every window there were beauties to be seen' (246). The
interior of Pemberley, with its lofty and handsome rooms, and
furniture which is 'neither gaudy nor uselessly fine' (246), contributes further to the sense of proper proportion, dignity and taste.

Given the contrasts between retainers and estates, it is hardly
surprising that the owners of Rosings and Pemberley, to whom
Elizabeth is next introduced, should be very different. Lady
Catherine de Bourgh, as Elizabeth anticipates, possesses neither

'extraordinary talents [n] or miraculous virtue' and depends for her prestige on 'the mere stateliness of money and rank' (161). As hostess, it is her duty to set her guests at their ease. However, far from acknowledging this obligation, she treats them in a manner designed to make them fully aware of their inferior rank, and obviously expects the kind of sycophantic response she receives from Mr Collins and Sir William Lucas at dinner:

> He carved, and ate, and praised with delighted alacrity; and every dish was commended, first by him, and then by Sir William, who was now enough recovered to echo whatever his son-in-law said, in a manner which Elizabeth wondered Lady Catherine could bear. But Lady Catherine seemed gratified by their excessive admiration, and gave most gracious smiles.   (163)

A sense of superiority also characterises Lady Catherine's conversational mode. The guests are relieved of any responsibility to initiate or even to participate in conversation. Their task is simply to listen and be informed as Lady Catherine pronounces authoritatively on a variety of subjects:

> When the ladies returned to the drawing room, there was little to be done but to hear Lady Catherine talk, which she did without any intermission till coffee came in, delivering her opinion on every subject in so decisive a manner as proved that she was not used to have her judgment controverted.   (163)

The god-like role she assumes here is even more evident at the end of the evening when 'the party . . . gathered round the fire to hear Lady Catherine determine what weather they were to have on the morrow' (166).

Further acquaintance soon reveals to Elizabeth that a similar sense of absolute authority characterises Lady Catherine's behaviour even beyond the confines of her own house. During visits to the Hunsford parsonage she presumes to comment on all aspects of Mrs Collins' housekeeping, and she uses her traditional position as leader of the local community as an excuse for interfering in the lives of the villagers:

> Elizabeth soon perceived that though this great lady was not in

the commission of the peace for the county, she was a most active magistrate in her own parish, the minutest concerns of which were carried to her by Mr Collins; and whenever any of the cottagers were disposed to be quarrelsome, discontented or too poor, she sallied forth into the village to settle their differences, silence their complaints, and scold them into harmony and plenty.   (169)

Neo-feudal arrogance, however, is not the mark of all aristocrats, and Darcy greets his guests, uninvited though they are, in a very different style. Even though he is embarrassed to meet Elizabeth, Darcy nevertheless makes 'civil inquiries after her family' (251), and conducts himself with extreme modesty: 'Never in her life had she seen his manners so little dignified, never had he spoken with such gentleness' (252). As an acknowledgement of Elizabeth's worth, Darcy expresses a wish to introduce her to his sister, thereby paying her 'a compliment of the highest kind' (257). 'Civility' (254) also characterises Darcy's reaction to the Gardiners, even after he learns that they are in trade. Such good manners suggest that the needs of his guests, rather than his own importance, are uppermost in Darcy's mind, and he performs two acts that confirm this impression. When Mr Gardiner expresses an interest in angling, Darcy immediately invites him to fish at Pemberley; and when he observes that Mrs Gardiner is tired, he presses her to take refreshments in his house. In their review of Darcy's behaviour, the Gardiners declare him to be 'perfectly well behaved, polite, and unassuming' and 'really attentive' (257).

Darcy is given a similar lesson in middle-class *mores* by the contrast between the manners of Collins and Sir William Lucas at Rosings, and the Gardiners at Pemberley. For a man such as Darcy, whose sense of human dignity is keenly developed, the clownish grovelling of Mr Collins and Sir William Lucas is perhaps even more offensive than the aggressive rudeness of Mrs Bennet. In any case, it cannot help but confirm his conviction that middle-class behaviour fails to serve the proper ends of polite intercourse. Far from contributing to an atmosphere of harmony and mutual respect, Collins and Sir William, as we have already seen, succeed only in encouraging Lady Catherine to indulge in further displays of overweening vanity.

The Gardiners' acquaintance with the aristocracy can hardly be more extensive than Sir William Lucas'. But they realise that there are certain absolute standards of politeness, and are thus able to greet Darcy with a proper mixture of dignity and respect: 'She listened most attentively to all that passed between them, and gloried in every expression, every sentence of her uncle, which marked his intelligence, his taste, or his good manners' (255). Mr Gardiner does not demean himself by expressing awe at the grandeur of his companion, but rather turns the conversation to fishing, a topic he can anticipate will be of mutual interest to himself and to the owner of well-stocked streams. At the same time, the Gardiners do not let the notice of a great gentleman go to their heads. Whereas Collins grasps at every crumb of attention Lady Catherine lets fall his way, they are careful to ensure that a proper distance is maintained. Therefore, when Darcy invites them to enter his house, they politely refuse.

The two visits, then, contribute greatly to the social education of Elizabeth and Darcy. Elizabeth learns that while a sense of their own importance does make some aristocrats unpleasantly condescending in their relationships with their 'inferiors' and neglectful of their social obligations, nevertheless this is not true of the group as a whole. Life at Pemberley is characterised by a concern for others and an attention to duty which operate on such a grand scale that Elizabeth at last becomes aware that the aristocrat has good reason to be proud. The limitations of Darcy's stereotypes are exposed with equal thoroughness. The middle class is more than Mr Collins and Sir William Lucas, and to label it as improper and vulgar is to do an injustice to people like the Gardiners, who not only know their duty but can perform it like 'people of fashion' (255).

This social enlightenment has profound consequences for Darcy and Elizabeth's relationship, and these can be best demonstrated by examining the contrasting patterns of interaction that characterise their encounters at Rosings and Pemberley. Elizabeth's poor opinion of the aristocracy is confirmed by acquaintance with Lady Catherine and by the revelation that Darcy effected the separation between Bingley and Jane: '[Darcy's] pride, she was convinced, would receive a deeper wound from the want of importance in his friend's connections, than from their want of sense; and she was quite decided at last, that he had been partly governed by this worst kind of pride' (187). Similarly, further contact with the middle class does not make Darcy any more ready to admit that Elizabeth's virtues owe anything to her background: '*You* cannot have a right to such very strong local attachment. *You* cannot have been always at

Longbourn' (179). Consequently, their meetings at Rosings continue to follow a pattern of approach and rejection.

Darcy quite literally draws near to Elizabeth during an evening at Rosings, but she is unwilling to acknowledge his claims to attention, and greets him with an arch and hostile comment:

> You mean to frighten me, Mr Darcy, by coming in all this state to hear me? But I will not be alarmed though your sister *does* play so well. There is stubbornness about me that never can bear to be frightened at the will of others. My courage always rises with every attempt to intimidate me.   (174)

Darcy, however, fails to heed the clear hint that Elizabeth still regards him as a snob, and continues in his efforts to engage her in conversation. Elizabeth consequently becomes more directly aggressive, and tries to embarrass Darcy by resurrecting her old grievance about his refusal to dance at the Meryton ball. Darcy sidesteps the implicit, and quite accurate, charge that he behaved snobbishly on that occasion, and pleads diffidence and shyness in conversation with new people; but Elizabeth refuses to be placated. Skilfully changing the point of attack, she argues that it is his duty to develop social graces:

> 'I certainly have not the talent which some people possess, ' said Darcy, 'of conversing easily with those I have never seen before . . .'
> 'My fingers,' said Elizabeth, 'do not move over this instrument in the masterly manner which I see so many women's do . . . But then I have always supposed it to be my own fault—because I would not take the trouble of practising.'   (175)

Her advice is good, but her aim is to rebuff Darcy's present advance rather than to improve his future conduct.

Darcy's subsequent approaches are no more successful. Elizabeth receives his first visit to the parsonage politely enough, but by refusing to believe that it was inspired by anything more than boredom (180), she deprives his overture of friendship of its significance. Further visits in company with Colonel Fitzwilliam merely convince Elizabeth that Darcy is inferior to his cousin. While he continues to place himself in her presence whenever possible, failure to establish communication with someone he now loves deeply increasingly incapacitates Darcy:

> More than once did Elizabeth in her ramble within the Park, unexpectedly meet Mr Darcy.—She felt all the perverseness of the mischance that should bring him where no one else was brought; and to prevent its ever happening again, took care to inform him at first, that it was a favourite haunt of hers.—How it could occur a second time therefore was very odd!—Yet it did, and even a third. It seemed like wilful ill-nature, or a voluntary penance, for on these occasions it was not merely a few formal enquiries and an awkward pause and then away, but he actually thought it necessary to turn back and walk with her. He never said a great deal, nor did she give herself the trouble of talking or of listening much.   (182)

Thus, no foundation of mutual understanding has been laid before Darcy makes the ultimate gesture of communication by asking Elizabeth to marry him. His hopes of success are based on recognition of a certain receptiveness to his approaches. However, Elizabeth is not conscious of any feelings other than dislike and, since his proposal is phrased in a condescending and almost unwilling way that proves he has not overcome his original prejudices, she once again rejects him. The only difference is that now she makes her objections explicit:

> From the very beginning, from the first moment I may almost say, of my acquaintance with you, your manners impressing me with the fullest belief of your arrogance, your conceit, and your selfish disdain of the feelings of others, were such as to form that ground-work of disapprobation, on which succeeding events have built so immoveable a dislike; and I had not known you a month before I felt that you were the last man in the world whom I could ever be prevailed on to marry.   (193)

The tone of finality here is even greater than when Elizabeth and Darcy parted at the Netherfield ball. Yet, in their next series of meetings at Pemberley, a pattern of approach and acceptance prevails. The seed of this change is contained, paradoxically, within what seems to be the most complete of all rejections. Elizabeth's rebuke and Darcy's subsequent explanation force each to give fresh consideration to the validity of his prejudices. Reassessment is rapidly completed by exposure to the best of each other's worlds at Pemberley, and Elizabeth is at last able to acknowledge her feelings for Darcy.

Emotional liberation begins with Elizabeth's first view of Pemberley: 'at that moment she felt, that to be mistress of Pemberley might be something!' (245). And it is completed by the realisation that Darcy will accept her uncle and aunt, whom she had believed would be lost to her (245) if she married him. Darcy's approaches at last meet with success. Elizabeth agrees to receive his sister, then to dine at Pemberley (263–4), and finally she makes a spontaneous approach to Darcy by returning Georgiana's visit (267). Whereas emotional immaturity blinded Elizabeth to the significance of Darcy's earlier ritual manoeuvrings, she is now fully aware of the significance of his approaches and of her own response:

> He who, she had been persuaded, would avoid her as his greatest enemy, seemed, on this accidental meeting, most eager to preserve the acquaintance, and without any indelicate display of regard, or any peculiarity of manner, where their two selves only were concerned, was soliciting the good opinion of her friends, and bent on making her known to his sister. Such a change in a man of so much pride, excited not only astonishment but gratitude—for to love, ardent love, it must be attributed; and as such its impression on her was of a sort to be encouraged, as by no means unpleasing, though it could not be exactly defined. She respected, she esteemed, she was grateful to him, she felt a real interest in his welfare.   (265–6)

After the morning visit to Pemberley, Darcy makes a public declaration of his admiration for Elizabeth: 'it is many months since I have considered her as one of the handsomest women of my acquaintance' (271). Marriage now seems close, but before Elizabeth can fulfill her dinner engagement she is called away from Pemberley by the news of Lydia's elopement. Jane Austen delays her main action in this way so that Darcy's acceptance of the Bennets might be fully tested. He must endure three trials, each of which ends in a marriage, the third being his own. The first, and most difficult, arises directly out of the elopement. Since mere impropriety had been enough to evoke Darcy's scorn earlier, the gross immorality of Lydia's actions clearly puts an intense strain on his revised opinion of the middle class. However, helped by the feeling that he is partly to blame himself, for keeping his knowledge of Wickham's previous misdemeanours secret, Darcy is able to avoid drawing general social conclusions from Lydia's behaviour. Thus, far from rejecting the Bennet family, he demonstrates an active concern with their affairs by becoming involved in the search for Lydia and Wickham, and by helping to arrange their marriage.

Although not as severe as the first, the other two tests are nevertheless trying for a man as proud as Darcy. Recognition that he has been wrong to reject the Bennet family in its entirety because of the failings of some of its members involves Darcy in the humiliating task of telling Bingley that he should not have persuaded him to separate from Jane. His reward, however, is Bingley and Jane's rapid renewal of affection and engagement to marry. Finally, Darcy must atone for his mistreatment of Mrs Bennet. This he does during a dinner at Longbourn. Mrs Bennet does not make things easy for Darcy. Under her tutelage, the party is conducted with that lack of regard for conversational opportunities that Darcy hates, especially as it means he has almost no chance to talk to Elizabeth:

> The gentlemen came; and she thought he looked as if he would have answered her hopes; but alas! the ladies had crowded round the table, where Miss Bennet was making tea, and Elizabeth pouring out the coffee, in so close a confederacy, that there was not a single vacancy near her, which would admit of a chair . . . When the tea-things were removed, and the card tables placed, the ladies all rose, and Elizabeth was then hoping to be soon joined by him, when all her views were overthrown, by seeing him fall a victim to her mother's rapacity for whist players.   (341–2)

Furthermore, Mrs Bennet makes no attempt to conceal her long-standing resentment of Darcy, and when she sits next to him she is ungracious (340). In such circumstances, Darcy does well simply to avoid rudeness, but in fact, as Mrs Bennet admits, he even manages to pay her a few conventional compliments: 'The soup was fifty times better than what we had the Lucas's last week; and even Mr Darcy acknowledged, that the partridges were remarkably well done' (342). Darcy's forbearance is rewarded with yet another marriage. A few days later he renews his proposal, and is accepted by Elizabeth. Thus by the time the sequence of marriages has been completed, all conflicts and misunderstandings have been resolved, and Darcy and Elizabeth have been placed firmly at the centre of a world characterised by a sense of order and harmony.

This union of aristocracy and gentry-middle class is not achieved easily; but it is possible, Jane Austen claims, because, despite their different social roles, the two groups are united by a shared ideal of concern for others. As Elizabeth tells Lady Catherine: 'In marrying your nephew, I should not consider myself as quitting that sphere. He is a gentleman; I am a gentleman's daughter; so far we are equal' (356). The moral strength of Pemberley, then, is not based so much on the exclusion of disruptive forces, although Lydia and Wickham are banned, but on the inclusion of responsible people from the aristocracy, the gentry and the middle class. Darcy and Elizabeth are resident, Bingley and Jane live close by, and the Gardiners from Gracechurch Street are the most welcome of visitors: 'With the Gardiners, they were always on the most intimate terms. Darcy, as well as Elizabeth, really loved them' (388).

This vision of order and harmony is not expressed thematically until marriage resolves Elizabeth and Darcy's conflicts. However, it is implicit throughout in the novel's highly-patterned structure, based on the dance invitation motif, the visits to Rosings and Pemberley, the final sequence of marriages, and an overall pattern of approach-rejection-acceptance. Form and content are truly one in *Pride and Prejudice*.[6]

4 Mansfield Park

If her presentation of great houses is anything to go by, Jane Austen began to lose confidence in English landed society some time between the writing of *Pride and Prejudice* and *Mansfield Park*. In their externals, Mansfield Park and Sotherton are suggestive of much the same ideals as Pemberley. The sheer bulk of the houses and the spaciousness of their parks underline the authority of the land-owners; the careful cultivation of nature, whether it be the stream at Pemberley, or the avenue of trees at Sotherton, serves as a reminder of the organic principles upon which society is founded; and the conduct of daily life with its 'consideration of times and seasons' (383) reinforces values such as 'elegance, propriety, regularity, harmony' (391).[1] However, whereas what Pemberley symbolises is made into a reality by Darcy, neither Sir Thomas Bertram nor Rushworth does more than keep up appearances.

In Sir Thomas' case it is not ignorance of proper standards, but a kind of shyness or even apathy, that often prevents him questioning what might lie beneath an orderly surface. Sir Thomas is, for example, 'a truly anxious father', but 'the reserve of his manner' (19) makes it hard for him to establish intimate relationships with his children, and he tends to avoid situations that would involve him in struggling to overcome this reserve. Therefore, simply because they appear to be 'in person, manner, and accomplishments every thing that could satisfy his anxiety' (20), he refrains from question-ing the quality of Maria and Julia's education. As a result he fails to uncover their deficiencies in 'self-knowledge, generosity, and humility' (19). Similarly, when he returns from Antigua, Sir Thomas puts an end to the theatricals, and restores order to his house, but makes no attempt to investigate the cause of his children's anarchic behaviour:

> He did not enter into any remonstrance with his other children:
> he was more willing to believe they felt their error, than to run the
> risk of investigation. The reproof of an immediate conclusion of

93

every thing, the sweep of every preparation would be sufficient.   (187)

Not even diffidence, however, can be pleaded in defence of Sir Thomas' response to his recognition that Maria is indifferent to her fiancé, Rushworth. Concern for his daughter's happiness forces Sir Thomas to question her motives, but so 'very proper' (203) an alliance with a man who is of high rank, wealthy, a close neighbour, and the right political colour, is too attractive for him to pursue the matter very far: 'Sir Thomas was satisfied; too glad to be satisfied perhaps to urge the matter quite so far as his judgment might have dictated to others. It was an alliance which he could not have relinquished without pain' (201). Whereas Sir Thomas Bertram fails to ensure that reality matches appearance, Rushworth is too foolish even to see that anything might exist beyond appearance. Strictest 'etiquette' (203) characterises the conduct of all affairs at Sotherton, but, as in his inability to see any significance in the cessation of the custom of family prayers, and in his readiness to cut down the avenue of trees, Rushworth reveals a moral idiocy about anything more substantial.

Because of the deficiencies of its leaders, landed society in *Mansfield Park* is ripe for corruption. Maria and Julia Bertram and their brother Tom are particularly vulnerable. None of them has been taught the active principles that should underlie a concern with propriety. Therefore, they consider the rather rigid style of correct behaviour upon which Sir Thomas insists as a pointless and stifling form of oppression, and are ready to accept anything that promises 'air and liberty' (90). Edmund is a much more serious person, and has an excellent theoretical knowledge of Mansfield values. His analysis of the role of the clergyman, for example, contains within it a brilliant justification of a rural society based on the unit of the small community (93). Nevertheless, Edmund is in scarcely less danger. Sir Thomas' poor example has left him insufficiently informed about the practical ways in which manners are connected with morals, and this, combined with the dullness of life at Mansfield Park, makes him too susceptible to the attractions of the merely charming performance.

The situation thus created, in which great value is attached to lively manners, and moral deficiencies are either excused or even welcomed, is one that the Crawfords are well equipped to exploit. Their London ethics threaten everything that Mansfield Park represents. However, they possess exactly the kind of vivacity and wit for which all the Bertram children are looking, and it soon becomes very likely that Mansfield will yield itself up to them. Jane Austen leaves little doubt as to what will be the consequences of this. Neither Crawford has much sympathy with the country-house ideal. Henry, for example, pays so little attention to his estate at Everingham that it has come under the control of a corrupt steward, and Mary dislikes nature and is scornful of religion. Their real allegiance is to the new urban world in which 'every thing is to be got with money' (58) and in which 'crowds' (93) and bustle have replaced face-to-face contacts and 'peace and tranquillity' (391). Should Mansfield Park model itself along these lines and make money its only source of value, it will suffer a similar loss of humanity. Like Mary Crawford's London set, the rich will become 'cold-hearted' through 'habits of wealth' (421), and, like the Prices in Portsmouth, the poor will be degraded by lack of money.[2]

Only one member of the Bertram family, the poor relation Fanny Price, has sufficient grasp of Mansfield ideals, and understanding of the relationship of manners to morals, to remain impervious to the influence of the Crawfords. Therefore, the survival of the old order depends entirely on her. Unfortunately, Fanny is in many ways ill-equipped for this task. Natural reticence, physical weakness, uncertainty about her position within the family, and exclusion from the Bertrams' social life, have combined to make Fanny an extremely timid and passive person, a 'creepmouse' (145) incapable of asserting herself in the social context. Yet unadorned virtue has little attraction for the frivolous Maria, Julia and Tom, and soon palls even for Edmund, once he experiences the charms of Mary Crawford. Fanny's repeated attempts to be 'of service' (432) may be admirable but, since they usually take the form of fetching and carrying for Lady Bertram and Mrs Norris, they do little more than convince the younger Bertrams that she is a kind of superior servant who can be conveniently ignored. If her morality is to become attractive to them it must be cloaked in a pleasing social perform-ance.[3] Only with an improvement in her manners, then, can Fanny hope to move out of the little white attic and the east room, and become guardian of the whole house or, as Fleishman puts it, develop from the position of ward to that of warden.[4]

The main business of the formal social occasion in *Mansfield Park* is to trace the way in which Fanny effects this transition in her polite performance. The process can be broken down into three stages, each of which is structured around a pattern of movement that reflects the current state of Fanny's relationship to her society. In the first part of the novel, Fanny remains passive, and is frequently left on the edge of the circle of involvement as the Bertrams move away from her and towards the Crawfords. Only Edmund introduces a variation into the pattern because he has sufficient sympathy for Fanny's morality to gravitate repeatedly towards her, before being pulled away by the force of Mary Crawford's charm. In the second part, Fanny becomes more active and by attracting others towards her, most notably Sir Thomas Bertram and Henry Crawford, is able to progress towards the centre of her social circle. In the third part, however, she must become still again, because further movement can be achieved only by giving in to attempts to make her marry Henry Crawford. The pattern of forces at work here, however, is very different from that which operated in the first part of the novel. Then Fanny was left isolated and morally impotent as others moved away from her. Now she is the centre of attention, and, if she can remain still in the face of concerted pressure to make her move, she will force Henry Crawford to expose his moral deficiencies and thus bring about the salvation of Mansfield Park.[5]

The extent to which Fanny's lack of charm limits her sphere of moral influence becomes very evident during the first formal encounter between the Bertrams and the Crawfords. The evening's main topic of conversation is improvements, and the positions taken by the participants leave little doubt of their relative worth. The aversion which Fanny expresses towards Rushworth's plan to destroy the avenue of trees leading up to Sotherton reveals her preference for that which has developed organically over that which is drastically innovative, and thus places her solidly in the conservative tradition. Mary Crawford, who, significantly, is seated 'exactly opposite' (56) Fanny, states a willingness to accept any improvements that can be purchased, but not to endure the business of improving: 'I should be most thankful to any Mr Repton who would undertake it, and give me as much beauty as he could for my money; and I should never look at it, till it was complete' (57). As is the case here, so in general, Mary tends to assume that money rather than personal commitment is all that is needed to achieve the good things in life. Henry Crawford, on the other hand, as he admits himself, gains pleasure from the process of improvement rather than from its results. The project of improving his estate at Everingham involved him totally, but once it was completed, he lost all interest. The larger implications of Henry Crawford's attitude to improvements are defined by his own words: 'My plan was laid at Westminster—a little altered perhaps at Cambridge, but at one and twenty executed. I am inclined to envy Mr Rushworth for having so much happiness yet before him. I have been a devourer of my own' (61). In their different ways, both Mary and Henry Crawford reveal a stunted comprehension of the individual's moral relationship with time, she trying to deny that the past need play any role in shaping the present, and he involving himself totally in the present at the expense of future considerations. Only Fanny views life in the correct way as a continuum of past, present and future.

Mary's materialism and its incompatibility with the values of the old order are further exposed during a conversation about the delivery of her harp. For Mary, the transportation of the harp from Northampton to Mansfield is a matter of business pure and simple, and should be handled by direct enquiry and by an appropriate disposition of money. In the country, however, business methods have not yet taken precedence over traditional ways of doing things, and Mary is astonished to discover that she must rely on a chain of personal connections to discover the whereabouts of her harp, and that the possibility of a quick profit is not sufficient to persuade the farmers to divert their carts from the harvest (57–8). Money plays such a central part in Mary Crawford's system of values that when Edmund, doubtless inspired by recent victories over the French, describes the navy as 'a noble profession,' she replies: 'Yes, the profession is well enough under two circumstances; if it make the fortune, and there be discretion in spending it' (60). To this crude materialism Mary Crawford occasionally adds vulgarity, as in her joke about 'Rears, and Vices' (60).

However, clear as the moral distinctions between Fanny and the Crawfords may be, they mean little to any of the Bertrams, with the partial exception of Edmund. Mary and Henry have been witty and charming; Fanny has been dull as usual. Therefore, when the question of a visit to Sotherton arises at the end of the evening, no one but Edmund disagrees with Mrs Norris' decision that Fanny should be excluded from the party (62). Even Edmund, however, does not go so far as to suggest that the Crawfords are not fit company for the Bertrams, and there are clear signs that for him Mary Crawford's liveliness goes a long way towards compensating for her moral deficiencies. In reviewing the conduct of the guests, Edmund begins by calling upon Fanny to confirm his view that Mary Crawford's behaviour was 'very wrong—very indecorous' (63). It is not long though before Edmund ceases to express moral outrage, and he concludes his comments by excusing what he initially condemned:

> The right of a lively mind, Fanny, seizing whatever may contribute to its own amusement or that of others; perfectly allowable, when untinctured by ill humour or roughness; and there is not a shadow of either in the countenance or manner of Miss Crawford.   (64)

Patterns of movement are thus suggested in this scene which can only intensify so long as Fanny has nothing better than passive virtue to set against the charms of the Crawfords. Maria, Julia and Tom will inevitably continue to gravitate away from what is silent, still and, to them, almost invisible, and towards what is talkative and lively. Edmund, even though he is by no means blind to Fanny's worth, will put an increasing value on Mary Crawford's attractive manners. Fanny, as a result, will become ever more isolated and thus powerless to prevent the corruption of the old order.

By the time of the Sotherton visit the patterns have achieved sharp definition. Again, there can be little doubt that the others should look to Fanny for guidance. Apart from Edmund, neither the visitors to Sotherton nor its owners can begin to match Fanny's understanding of what this great house, 'built in Elizabeth's time' (56), stands for. Rushworth and his mother are punctilious about questions of etiquette; the guests are 'welcomed by him with due attention' and eat a lunch characterised by 'abundance and elegance' (84). However, they have little grasp of anything more substantial. The history of the house is something that Mrs Rushworth has learnt simply that she might be able to guide and impress visitors, and in no sense does she regard herself as part of a living tradition. The state of the cottages in the village, which Maria describes as a 'disgrace' (82), the distance of the church from the house, and the redundancy of the family chapel suggest that Rushworth neglects both his secular and religious obligations to the community under his charge. For Maria and Julia Bertram Sotherton is, like their own house, nothing more than a place of confinement, 'a dismal old prison' (53), from which they must escape as soon as possible (90). The Crawfords are equally unsympathetic to Sotherton; Henry wants to introduce improvements that will change its entire character, and Mary judges the tour of the house 'the greatest bore in the world' (96). Fanny, by contrast, is eager to learn all she can about the house and its history, and through her imagination its traditions reassume some of their former vitality: 'There is something in a chapel and chaplain so much in character with a great house, with one's ideas of what such a household should be! A whole family assembling regularly for the purpose of prayer, is fine!' (86).

However the Bertrams' relationships owe more to considerations of charm than ethics, and demonstrations of moral superiority go for little with them. Fanny's attractions are so minimal compared to Henry Crawford's that the Bertram sisters scarcely acknowledge her presence. Throughout the drive to Sotherton they vie for Henry's attention, and Fanny 'was not often invited to join in the conversation of the others' (80). In the wilderness Maria seats herself between Rushworth and Henry Crawford and directs all her comments to them as if Fanny were not there. When Fanny finally forces herself into Maria's attention, by warning her of the dangers, more moral than literal, of crossing the ha-ha, she is casually dismissed: 'Her cousin was safe on the other side, while these words were spoken, and smiling with all the good-humour of success, she said, "Thank you, my dear Fanny, but I and my gown are alive and well, and so good bye" ' (100). Because he has sufficient moral sense to recognise Fanny's worth, Edmund does not reject her so readily. Indeed, it is because of his efforts that she is included in the party, and during conversations in the chapel (86–8) and on the edge of the wilderness (91–4), Edmund is united with Fanny against Mary Crawford. Yet, even though the lack of respect for family worship and the clergy expressed by Mary reveals a serious lack of correct principles, she conducts herself in so 'light and lively' (81) a manner that Edmund has no hesitation in choosing to take a 'serpentine course' (94) with her deep into the wilderness, rather than sit by the tired Fanny. With the desertion of the one person who is inclined to be sympathetic to her moral position, Fanny is 'left to her solitude' (100).

The triangle of forces in which Edmund is pulled towards Fanny by respect for her moral seriousness before yielding up to the charms of Mary Crawford comes into operation again during an evening party at Mansfield.[6] Mary continues her attack on the clergy, this time going so far as to hint that only the prospect of an immediate living and a subsequent life of idleness could have motivated Edmund to enter such an ignoble profession. And once more she finds herself faced with the combined opposition of Fanny and Edmund. Fanny's display of good sense and firm principles is so impressive on this occasion that Edmund stays beside her even after Mary Crawford joins the main party in a glee. It is not long, however, before Mary Crawford and the glee prove to be more attractive than Fanny's raptures on the stars:

> The glee began. 'We will stay till this is finished, Fanny,' said he, turning his back on the window; and as it advanced, she had the mortification of seeing him advance too, moving forward by gentle degrees towards the instrument, and when it ceased, he was close by the singers, among the most urgent in requesting to hear the glee again.   (113)

Since Maria and Julia, as usual, have no attention to spare for Fanny, Edmund's defection again ensures her complete isolation and moral impotence: 'Fanny sighed alone at the window' (113).

Fanny is equally unsuccessful during an impromptu ball held at Mansfield Park because, after dancing twice with Edmund, she loses him to Mary Crawford and finds herself without a partner. The relative positioning of the characters during the dance further underlines that once she is deprived of Edmund's companionship, Fanny becomes isolated from the Mansfield group and is unable to influence its moral direction. Taking the dance floor as a symbol for the social world, we are presented with a tableau in which Fanny alone is placed outside the circle of involvement. Inside it extremely dangerous activities are going on unchecked, for Maria, technically Rushworth's partner, is trying to attract Henry Crawford away from Julia:

> it was while all the other young people were dancing, and she sitting, most unwillingly, among the chaperons at the fire . . .
>
> Miss Bertram did indeed look happy, her eyes were sparkling with pleasure, and she was speaking with great animation, for Julia and her partner, Mr Crawford, were close to her; they were all in a cluster together.'   (116–17)

Defining Fanny's task in terms of this dance metaphor, she needs to become sufficiently attractive to be invited onto the floor. However, she must find a partner who chooses her for better reasons than those which finally motivate Tom on this occasion. By electing to dance with Fanny rather than suffer the greater evil of playing cards with Mrs Norris, Tom simply reconfirms that, to the Bertrams, she is little more than an object of convenience, and thereby stresses rather than alleviates her real isolation.

Because the salvation of Mansfield Park is so dependent on Fanny's ability to become involved in society, the theatricals must be regarded as the novel's turning point. Their immediate effect is, of course, hardly promising. Inspired by yet another intruder, the idle aristocrat, Yates, the theatricals increase existing ills and lead the Bertrams into new improprieties. By allowing himself to become involved, Edmund is particularly responsible for the atmosphere of anarchy that prevails. Initially, Edmund had joined Fanny in objecting to the theatricals. However, the prospect of acting opposite Mary Crawford finally persuades him to move away from her once again and to take a role. This 'descent' 'from that moral elevation which he had maintained before' (158) gives Tom and Maria an excuse to cast off the last vestiges of restraint. Tom allows the 'darling project' (158) to occupy his entire attention, and ignores his responsibility, as senior Bertram in Sir Thomas' absence, to attend to the behaviour of his sisters (163); Maria pursues her flirtation with Henry Crawford so furiously that even the obtuse Rushworth becomes concerned. With Edmund's desertion, Fanny is again completely isolated and although she is acutely aware of the selfishness, impropriety, expense, bustle, and noise that characterise the theatricals, she is unable to do anything to influence the conduct of the Bertrams or the Crawfords. As usual she substitutes attempts to be useful for real involvement, but none of the generosity she displays in serving as prompter, listening to complaints or teaching Rushworth his lines, rubs off on her companions.

What is hopeful, however, is Fanny's reaction to her isolation. Morally she has no reason to doubt the wisdom of her refusal to become involved by taking the part of the Cottager's Wife. The theatricals are an offence against Sir Thomas and his home, and the particular play, *Lovers' Vows* combines political radicalism with sexual permissiveness.[7] Yet Fanny is troubled by her decision because, for the first time, she begins to see the necessity of participating in society. Exclusion has always been painful to Fanny, but previously she has been able to find consolation in a private world of reading, nature and correspondence with her brother William. On this occasion, however, she is so aware that the consequence and perhaps even the love she wants so badly are reserved for those who are willing to be socially active that she is unable to shift her attention away from a pursuit in which all are included but herself:

> She alone was sad and insignificant; she had no share in any thing; she might go or stay, she might be in the midst of their noise, or retreat from it to the solitude of the East room, without being seen or missed. She could almost think any thing would have been preferable to this. Mrs Grant was of consequence; *her* good nature had honourable mention—her taste and her time were considered—her presence was wanted—she was sought for and attended, and praised; and Fanny was at first in some danger of envying her the character she had accepted.   (159–60)

This important change in perspective is symbolised by an episode which takes place in Fanny's room. The East room, with its books, its Romantic transparencies and its sketch of William's ship the *Antwerp* has served throughout the novel not only as a literal place of retreat for Fanny, but as an emblem of her private inner world. On this particular occasion, Fanny has retired into it to escape from the thoughts of the love scene that Edmund and Mary are to rehearse that evening. Escape, however, is not possible. Mary and Edmund seek out Fanny and rehearse the dreaded scene in front of her. By this symbolic means, Jane Austen underlines that Fanny has now become too conscious of the rewards of involvement to turn away from the social context, even when what is going on there is a source of pain to her.

Given Fanny's new impulse towards involvement, it is not surprising that, when it is offered her a second time, she agrees to take the part of Cottager's Wife. By joining the theatricals, Fanny is putting herself in moral danger. At the same time, though, she is assuming a position from which she may be able to exert some influence. Therefore, rather than seeing Sir Thomas' sudden return as providing Fanny with a lucky escape from impropriety, we should perhaps consider it as depriving her of her first opportunity to reconcile the demands of her conscience with the claims of the group.

Fanny, however, is soon able to begin fulfilling her social ambitions. The departure of Henry Crawford opens up a position for her at the Parsonage, where the bored Mary Crawford is eager for amusement and conversation; Maria's marriage leaves Lady Bertram in need of a companion, a role she quickly fills; and, most important, Sir Thomas begins to acknowledge her claims to be considered a part of the family and hence to be included more fully in its social life. When Lady Bertram and Mrs Norris try to prevent Fanny accepting an invitation to dine with the Grants, it is Sir Thomas who intervenes and ensures that she is allowed to attend. Moreover, he forestalls Mrs Norris' mean-minded attempts to deny her the carriage, thereby making certain that she goes in a style befitting a member of his family. This crucial development in Sir Thomas' attitude does not result from any great improvement in Fanny who, apart from a physical blossoming, is still very much the person she was before he left for Antigua. It is simply that Sir Thomas, wearied by his travels and financial troubles, has become very sensitive to the value of those retiring qualities which usually cause Fanny to be ignored.

Although Fanny's entry into society thus results more from luck than anything else, once given her chance she is able to take advantage of it. To be invited to social occasions in her own right is very different from tagging along behind Edmund, and Fanny's self confidence increases in proportion to the increased consequence granted her. The visit of William Price, who extends to her a love and sense of concern that she has never experienced in the Bertram household, contributes further to the improvement in Fanny's spirits. As a result, her social performance becomes much more lively and appealing, and the pattern which characterised social gatherings in the first part of the novel alters significantly. Edmund is too entangled with Mary Crawford to respond appropriately even to a more attractive Fanny, but others, most notably Sir Thomas and Henry Crawford, pay her increasing attention. And so, having nervously entered the social circle at the Grants' dinner party, Fanny is able to move rapidly towards its centre. Her arrival there is marked by a ball held in her honour at Mansfield Park, and by Henry Crawford's marriage proposal.

Fanny's reaction to the Grants' invitation shows that she has not forgotten what she learnt during the theatricals. Although she does not relish the prospect of seeing Edmund and Mary together, Fanny is fully appreciative of this rare opportunity for social involvement:

> Simple as such an engagement might appear in other eyes, it had
> novelty and importance in her's, for excepting the day at
> Sotherton, she had scarcely ever dined out before; and though
> now going only half a mile and only to three people, still it was
> dining out.   (219)

As yet, however, despite Sir Thomas' insistence that she be treated
as his niece, Fanny does not have enough sense of her own
importance to disagree with Mrs Norris' contention that she must
be 'lowest and last' (221), and her plans for the evening involve
nothing more ambitious than to 'sit silent and unattended to' (223).
In the event, though, Fanny does rather better than that.
Throughout dinner she takes no part in the conversation but,
perhaps inspired by her new sense of belonging to the Bertram
family, she is unable to remain silent when Henry Crawford laments
her uncle's role in halting the theatricals:

> He seemed determined to be answered; and Fanny, averting her
> face, said with a firmer tone than usual, 'As far as *I* am concerned,
> sir, I would not have delayed his return for a day. My uncle
> disapproved of it all so entirely when he did arrive, that in my
> opinion, every thing had gone quite far enough.'   (225)

This brief display of intense feeling (she had never before spoken 'so
angrily to any one' (225)), has a remarkable effect on Henry
Crawford. Suddenly he recognises Fanny as a person of unique
qualities rather than as an object to be ignored, and not only does he
quickly concur with her judgement but makes several determined
attempts to engage her in further conversation both then and later
in the evening. Even when he is talking to Edmund, Henry's
attention does not pass away entirely from Fanny: 'I shall make a
point of coming to Mansfield to hear you preach your first
sermon . . . When is it to be? Miss Price, will not you join me in
encouraging your cousin?' (227).

Fanny's performance at the Grants' next, and much larger,
dinner party is even more impressive. The rare opportunities for
'unchecked, equal, fearless intercourse' (234) provided by the visit
of her brother William have produced a great improvement in her
appearance and spirits, and she is much less reticent than on any
previous occasion. Thus, even though she has never played
Speculation before, Fanny is quite willing to take part in the game

that occupies the guests after dinner, and acquits herself well
enough that when she withdraws from the social circle in order to
talk to William, a new circle quickly forms around her:

> The chief of the party were now collected irregularly round the
> fire, and waiting the final break up. William and Fanny were the
> most detached. They remained together at the otherwise deserted
> card-table, talking very comfortably and not thinking of the rest,
> till some of the rest began to think of them.   (249)

Although Fanny is doubtless most satisfied by the interest Sir
Thomas shows in her, Henry Crawford's chair is in fact 'the first to
be given a direction towards' her (249), and it is his notice that has
helped to bring her into prominence throughout the evening. By
this time Henry, who has been tremendously impressed by 'the glow
of . . . cheek, the brightness of . . . eye' (235) that Fanny displays
when animated by William's company, is close to believing himself
in love, and he pays her attention whenever possible. During the
card game, for example, Henry sits next to Fanny and, by striving
'to inspirit her play, sharpen her avarice, and harden her heart'
(240), magnifies delicate charms that might otherwise have gone
unnoticed in the midst of such a boisterous activity as Speculation.
Similarly, when the subject of improvements comes up, Henry does
not allow himself to become so involved in his favourite topic as to
forget to include Fanny in the conversation: '*You* think with me, I
hope—(turning with a softened voice to Fanny).—Have you ever
seen the place?' (244). Later, Henry pays Fanny a polite compliment on her dancing that increases her prestige with Sir Thomas
Bertram, and, at the moment of departure, places her shawl around
her shoulders, with a 'prominent attention' (251).

This rapid improvement in Fanny's attitude towards and
performance during social gatherings reaches its climax with the
Mansfield ball, which Sir Thomas plans almost entirely in her
honour. Although she still lacks sufficient respect for herself to
realise that the ball is intended to mark her 'coming-out', Fanny
anticipates the opportunity for social involvement with pleasure,
and, plans to take part in an active if limited way:

> To dance without much observation or any extraordinary
> fatigue, to have strength and partners for about half the evening,
> to dance a little with Edmund, and not a great deal with Mr

Crawford, to see William enjoy himself, and be able to keep away from her aunt Norris, was the height of her ambition, and seemed to comprehend her greatest possibility of happiness.   (267)

Furthermore, the quality of her polite performance is now of sufficient importance to Fanny that she is willing to suffer Mary Crawford's company in order to get advice about her dress, and, despite her disapproval of Henry Crawford, she is glad to have secured him as a voluntary partner with whom to open the ball:

To be secure of a partner at first, was a most essential good—for the moment of beginning was now growing seriously near, and she so little understood her own claims as to think, that if Mr Crawford had not asked her, she must have been the last to be sought after, and should have received a partner only through a series of inquiry, and bustle, and interference which would have been terrible.   (274)

Clearly, Fanny has learnt the lessons of the Mansfield theatricals well, and the ball has sufficient claims in itself that not even Edmund's approval or support is necessary. Edmund is so caught up in problems of ordination and marriage that 'to engage [Mary Crawford] early for the first two dances' is 'the only preparation for the ball which he could enter into' (256), and he can express no more than the limpest of enthusiasm for what is to be the most important day of Fanny's life: 'Oh! yes, yes, and it will be a day of pleasure. It will all end right. I am only vexed for a moment' (268). Yet Fanny's spirits survive Edmund's dampening effect, and the ball increasingly comes to represent 'such an evening of pleasure before her!' (270).

By granting her the privilege of opening the ball, Sir Thomas forces Fanny into a much more prominent position than she would ever have chosen. Nevertheless, she is now well enough versed in the ways of society to put on an admirable performance:

Young, pretty, and gentle, however, she had no awkwardnesses that were not as good as graces, and there were few persons present that were not disposed to praise her. She was attractive, she was modest, she was Sir Thomas's niece, and she was soon said to be admired by Mr Crawford. It was enough to give her general favour. Sir Thomas himself was watching her progress down the dance with much complacency: he was proud of his niece.   (276)

This triumphant opening guarantees the success of the rest of the evening. Even if anyone is still inclined to underrate Fanny's claims, Sir Thomas' open display of admiration ensures that they pay her attention. Thus, Mary Crawford recognises that it would be politic 'to say something agreeable of Fanny' (276). On the whole, though, Fanny has displayed sufficient charms for this sponsorship to be unnecessary and, far from being short of partners as she had feared, she finds she is 'eagerly sought after' (278).

Fanny's performance at the ball completes Henry Crawford's infatuation, and shortly afterwards he asks her to marry him. Acceptance of this proposal would in many ways give Fanny the social consequence she so desperately needs, since Henry Crawford is a man who, in Sir Thomas' opinion, possesses both 'situation in life, fortune, and character,' and 'more than common agreeableness, with address and conversation pleasing to every body' (316). However, consequence arrived at in this way would be worthless to Fanny. To marry a man whom she does not love would destroy her chances of emotional fulfilment. Furthermore, Crawford is so corrupt he would prevent Fanny exercising any moral influence on her society. The implications of a match between Henry and Fanny are made clear by a part of the conversation that takes place during the game of Speculation at the Grants'. Crawford's account of how he lost his way and stumbled upon Thornton Lacey, which is to be Edmund's living, is emblematic of his attempt to usurp Edmund's emotional and moral role in Fanny's life. Henry Crawford's inability to comprehend the new moral code with which he is striving to associate himself is clearly revealed when he outlines his plans to 'improve' Thornton Lacey. These would serve, as Mary interprets them, 'to shut out the church, sink the clergyman' and produce in their place 'the respectable, elegant, modernized, and occasional residence of a man of independent fortune' (248). In spite of his affection for Fanny, and his temporary leaning towards her ethical position, we can be sure that once they were married Henry would try to bring about a similar improvement in her.

By putting her heroine in this situation, Jane Austen demonstrates that the equation she has been developing between social graces and moral influence is not a simple one. As a result of the attentions paid her by Sir Thomas Bertram and Henry Crawford, Fanny has at last established a firm foothold in society. Unfortunately, her most obvious way of progressing further is to follow the 'serpentine course' that would be opened up by marrying Henry. Fanny is far too wise not to be alert to the moral implications of taking such a direction and, attractive as a position of importance is to her, she is not much tempted to accept Henry's offer. However, now that she has come to the notice of her society, Fanny finds that her moral life is no longer entirely her own business. Having abandoned the sanctuary of an isolated inner life, as represented by the East room, she cannot simply retreat back into it when social involvement becomes difficult and unpleasant. Thus, Fanny's room provides her with only half-an-hour of comfort before Sir Thomas follows her into it and at once offers a reminder of the advantages of social consequence, by insisting that a fire be lit especially for her, and makes its problems very evident by questioning her right to refuse such a desirable offer. Since Sir Thomas' efforts are supported by Lady Bertram, Mary Crawford and even Edmund, what seemed at first to be a simple moral decision turns out to be a complex issue, involving Fanny's obligations not only to herself but also to her group. Fanny has always wanted to be of service to the Bertrams and to be loved by them. Now they make it clear that not only can she achieve both goals by marrying Henry Crawford, but that failure to comply with their wishes will be interpreted as an act of ingratitude and a demonstration of lack of affection. This makes it hard for Fanny to keep in view the greater long-term good that she can do the Bertrams by refusing Henry Crawford.

In a sense, then, Fanny's position is worse than ever, because she is now being tempted and pressured to exchange her most important values for prestige, security and wealth. However, in another, and finally more important, sense, it is better because she is at last the object of everyone's attention, and if she can remain true to her principles she will inevitably exercise a moral influence on the lives of those around her. Fanny's task, therefore, is to be still and to wait patiently until Henry Crawford either acquires the moral insight to respect her wishes or loses patience and passes on to a new interest. This stillness, which must be maintained at the centre of a world in which all around are united in their attempts to make her move, and, later, through a period of enforced exile, is clearly very different from her earlier isolated and morally impotent passivity.

There has been, then, a complete reversal in Fanny's situation.

Before, she lingered on the edge of the circle of involvement and was ignored. Now, she is at the centre and her task is to ignore. This is particularly evident during an evening at Mansfield Park. When Henry Crawford conducts an impromptu reading, he does it entirely for Fanny's benefit, and she tries to deny him her attention: 'Not a look, or an offer of help had Fanny given; not a syllable for or against. All her attention was for her work. She seemed determined to be interested by nothing else' (337). This proves to be extremely difficult, however, because Henry has chosen an activity at which he is particularly skilled and in which he knows Fanny will take pleasure. Furthermore, not even the tiniest gesture of interest will go unnoticed, because Edmund is so anxious to find out the state of Fanny's feelings that he concentrates on the audience rather than the performer. For all her efforts, Fanny fails the test:

> Edmund watched the progress of her attention, and was amused and gratified by seeing how she gradually slackened in the needle-work, which, at the beginning, seemed to occupy her totally; how it fell from her hand while she sat motionless over it— and at last, how the eyes which had appeared so studiously to avoid him throughout the day, were turned and fixed on Crawford, fixed on him for minutes, fixed on him in short till the attraction drew Crawford's upon her, and the book was closed, and the charm was broken.   (337)

As a result of this lapse, Edmund becomes convinced that Crawford's attentions are welcomed, and withdraws in order to give him the chance to approach Fanny directly:

> Crawford was instantly by her side again, intreating to know her meaning; and as Edmund perceived, by his drawing in a chair, and sitting down close by her, that it was to be a very thorough attack, that looks and undertones were to be well tried, he sank as quietly as possible into a corner, turned his back, and took up a newspaper.   (341–2)

Failure to remain absolutely still, then, has painful consequences because it exposes Fanny to extremely violent expressions of love and claims of constancy. However, such slight movements do not make it at all likely that she will accept Henry Crawford, and the *tête-à-tête* is brought to a conclusion in a manner that reminds us of the enormous task that Crawford has set himself. When Baddely enters with the tea things, he does not just represent a convenient intervention but rather, as is suggested by the formal tones in which Jane Austen describes him, that great weight of Mansfield tradition which buttresses Fanny's value system and which she is pledged to preserve: 'The solemn procession, headed by Baddely, of tea-board, urn, and cake bearers, made its appearance' (344). If Crawford is ever to succeed, this is what he must shift.

Given the important part played by Mansfield Park and its traditions in Fanny's rejection of Henry Crawford, Sir Thomas would seem to have made an astute move when he exiles her to Portsmouth. Without the physical presence of Mansfield to remind Fanny of what she is defending, it seems likely that she will be more easily influenced in Henry's favour. Sir Thomas, however, completely misjudges what Mansfield means to Fanny. It is his hope that the deprivations she will experience in the Price household will make Fanny more appreciative of 'the elegancies and luxuries of Mansfield Park', and consequently more ready to accept a man of 'good income' (369) who can offer her such things on a permanent basis. Instead, life in Portsmouth simply makes Fanny increasingly aware of the evil consequences of yielding up Mansfield values of 'consideration of times and seasons . . . regulation of subject, . . . propriety . . . attention towards every body' (383). Portsmouth, like London, with which Fanny also becomes intimately acquainted through the steady flow of letters she receives from Mary Crawford and Edmund, is a harbinger of what things will be like after the Mansfield Parks disappear and society becomes completely urbanised. The old rural order is based on principles of order and continuity which derive directly from the natural world in which it is located. These values are thus soon lost in places where nature intrudes only in the form of the sun's 'stifling, sickly glare' (439), and in London and Portsmouth 'nothing [is] of consequence but money' (436). This discovery Fanny makes in a very personal and rather painful way because she goes to Portsmouth hoping to experience the kind of love that she has always felt the lack of at Mansfield. What she finds, however, is that, deprived of the support of the paternalistic structures which operate in a society based on human considerations, her impoverished mother has become too caught up in the business of survival to have any emotional energy to spare for her returning daughter. The kind of quiet reflection which is necessary if the individual is to go beyond concern for the self is simply not possible amidst the 'noise, disorder, and impropriety' (388) in which economic circumstances compel Mrs Price to live. Thus, although Fanny arrives in Portsmouth quite ready to sacrifice 'manner' for 'love' (377), she soon comes to realise that, without manner, love is almost impossible. Mansfield's 'elegance, propriety, regularity, harmony' (391) do not guarantee that proper attention will be paid to the needs of the individual, but they do provide the conditions for such attention. In Portsmouth, the conditions simply do not exist, and the breakdown of human relationships is inevitable.[8]

Fanny conducts several experiments in the humanising of financial transactions. A dispute over the ownership of a silver knife, for example, causes recurring disagreements between Betsey and Susan, and Fanny finds that by buying another knife she can solve the problem. Similarly, by subscribing to a circulating library, Fanny is able to contribute to Susan's liberal education. Acquaintance with the manners of London, however, teaches Fanny that, in a society founded on the cash ethic, those who have managed to accumulate excess wealth do not commonly employ it in such ways. The rich value their money not because it enables them to be of service to others, but because it confers prestige on themselves. Thus, in spite of Rushworth's limitations as a human being, Maria is envied a marriage in which she has got 'her pennyworth for her penny' (394). As a consequence of adopting such an approach to experience, people become 'cold-hearted' and 'vain' (421), and Fanny is able to conclude that 'the influence of London [is] very much at war with all respectable attachments' (433).

Thus, so long as a return to Mansfield Park can be achieved only by accepting Henry Crawford, Fanny must contrive to remain still, this time in the less comfortable surroundings of the Prices' parlour. Her conviction that this is the only way of preventing Mansfield from becoming another Portsmouth or London is so firm that she remains faithful to it, even in the face of attempts by Henry Crawford to win her confidence that constitute at once the greatest performance of a man who has a chameleon ability to take on roles and the most opportunist enterprise of a man who has always lived by his wits. Although he is far too corrupt to live by Fanny's values, Crawford has sufficient moral sense to recognise what these values are, and during his visit to Portsmouth he passes himself as a very fair facsimile of the responsible country gentleman. During a walk to the Dockyard, for example, Crawford displays great consideration for the needs of Fanny, Susan and Captain Price. Price is something of a vulgarian, but Henry Crawford treats him with extreme civility, and seeks out subjects of common interest. At the same time, he is attentive to Susan and Fanny, and ensures that they are not left to fend for themselves through the streets of Portsmouth: 'at any crossing, or any crowd, when Mr Price was only calling out, "Come girls—come, Fan—come, Sue—take care of yourselves— keep a sharp look out," he would give them his particular attendance' (403). The role Henry Crawford is creating is by no means an impromptu one. Thus, he has recently paid a visit to his previously neglected estate at Everingham in order that it might serve as a prop in his performance as the responsible landowner:

> For her approbation, the particular reason of his going into Norfolk at all, at this unusual time of year, was given. It had been real business, relative to the renewal of a lease in which the welfare of a large and (he believed) industrious family was at stake . . . He had gone, had done even more good than he had foreseen, had been useful to more than his first plan had comprehended, and was now able to congratulate himself upon it, and to feel, that in performing a duty, he had secured agreeable recollections for his own mind.   (404)

As was the case in the Mansfield drawing room, Fanny is by no means unimpressed by the part Henry plays. At the end of his first day in Portsmouth, she judges him 'altogether improved' (406), and after he leaves 'she was quite persuaded of his being astonishingly more gentle, and regardful of others, than formerly' (413–14). Fanny, however, is too deeply imbued in the Mansfield approach to experience, whereby the cycle of the year rather than the moment is the basic unit of time, for such a brief performance, sparkling though it is, to alter her feelings. Far from moving towards an acceptance of Henry Crawford, Fanny simply hopes that as a consequence of his new awareness of her needs he will 'not much longer persevere in a suit so distressing to her' (414). Thus, even though Henry presses her in person and through his sister to return to Mansfield with him, Fanny prefers to remain in Portsmouth rather than 'be owing such felicity to persons in whose feelings and conduct . . . she saw so much to condemn' (436).

By remaining still, Fanny demands of Henry Crawford that he

display qualities of perseverance and moral commitment that are alien to his nature and to the world from which he derives. A situation is thus created which almost guarantees that, so long as Fanny does not die under the harsh conditions of life in Portsmouth, Mansfield Park will be saved. And, indeed, Crawford's patience soon runs out, and his attention is directed back to Maria, with whom he elopes. This elopement sets in motion a chain of events that leads to the complete moral re-ordering of Mansfield Park. Mary's cynical and worldly response to Henry's behaviour at last convinces Edmund that hers are the incurable faults 'of blunted delicacy and a corrupted, vitiated mind' (456); Sir Thomas finally becomes aware that his conduct as a parent has been gravely deficient; and even Julia and Tom begin to make efforts to correct their way of life. Other corrupting influences are rapidly dispelled as Mrs Norris leaves to keep her beloved Maria company in exile, and the Grants move to London. All that then remains is for Edmund, free at last to recognise his cousin's charms, to fall in love with and marry Fanny Price. After a short removal to Thornton Lacey, they inevitably take their place at Mansfield Parsonage, which becomes vacant with Dr Grant's convenient death. With this restoration of spiritual significance to the very place through which the Crawfords made their entry, the moral rebirth of Mansfield Park and the salvation of the old society is completed.

Fanny's ability to resist all efforts to make her marry Henry Crawford is ultimately responsible for the regeneration of Mansfield society. However, if she had not come to realise the importance of operating within the social context, and if she had not managed to develop a more attractive polite performance, Fanny would not have been given the chance to exercise her moral strength. To make this equation between charm and moral influence clear, Jane Austen structures the formal social occasions in *Mansfield Park* around three patterns of movement, which reflect the successive stages in Fanny's relationship with her society. Fanny begins and ends in a condition of stillness, but there is a period of movement in the middle sections of the novel that makes them very different in quality. At first, Fanny's firm morality has no influence on the direction of Mansfield life because the Bertrams find her dull and repeatedly move away from her. However, by daring to become socially involved, and by learning charm, she gradually progresses to the centre of her society. Having achieved a position in which others move towards rather than away from her, she can become still again and yet exercise a moral influence. In condemning Mary Crawford, then, *Mansfield Park* does not, as is sometimes supposed, condemn vitality and charm.[9] On the contrary, through its presentation of Fanny's development from passivity to stillness, it demonstrates that firm principles are worthless unless expressed through pleasing manners.

5 Emma

Highbury seems to have little in common with Mansfield Park. Whereas the Bertram family is rift by dissent, all the different divisions of Highbury society exist in a state of harmony and mutual esteem. To live there is, as Miss Bates says, to have your 'lot cast in a goodly heritage' (174) and to be 'blessed in [your] neighbours' (175). Mr Woodhouse's claims to attention are recognised not only within his own small circle, but by the entire community. When he needs companions while Emma visits the Coles, the services of Mrs Bates and Mrs Goddard are readily secured. Similarly, Perry is always on hand to minister to Mr Woodhouse's imaginary ailments. And even Hannah, the Westons' young servant, is careful not to bang doors during her visits to Hartfield. The leading families, in their turn, are equally attentive to the more real needs of less fortunate villagers. Mr Woodhouse, for example, gives the Bates' family a hind-quarter of pork, and Mr Knightley sends them the last of his apples, provides them with transportation to the Coles' dinner party and enquires whether he can be of service during his business trip to Kingston. Emma's concern extends even further down the social scale, and 'the distresses of the poor were as sure of relief from her personal attention and kindness, her counsel and her patience, as from her purse' (86). The good fortune of others is of sufficiently fundamental importance to Highbury society for Emma to be able to assure Frank Churchill that a purchase at the village shop will win him the regard of the entire community:

> I do admire your patriotism. You will be adored in Highbury. You were very popular before you came, because you were Mr Weston's son—but lay out half-a-guinea at Ford's, and your popularity will stand upon your own virtues.   (200)[1]

The kind of dissatisfaction with the *status quo* that makes Mansfield Park so amenable to corrupting outside influences clearly does not exist within the village of Highbury. Therefore, although

Mrs Elton's materialism and bourgeois vulgarity, and Frank Churchill's restless energy, make them potentially as dangerous as the Crawfords, neither is able to damage the community into which he intrudes. They are simply judged, found wanting and then tolerated. However, the very sense of order and contentment which makes Highbury appear so much more secure than Mansfield Park poses its own threat. Life in Highbury has become too comfortable, and the villagers tend to assume that nothing need change. The main symptom of this attitude is the almost complete cessation of organised social activity. The leading families do little formal entertaining and balls are no longer held at the Crown. As a result, relationships cease to develop, manners and morals go untested and become static, and there are insufficient opportunities for courtship and the necessary change which it produces in the form of marriage.[2]

The total atrophy which can result from this refusal to admit that the social organism must continually modify itself is epitomised by the village's leading citizen, Mr Woodhouse, who hates 'change of every kind' (7).[3] The slightest deviation from his normal daily routine, which is circumscribed by the boundaries of Hartfield, causes him considerable anxiety. The Bates' house, for example, is only a few hundred yards away from Hartfield down the main street of the village. However, Mr Woodhouse is not used to going there himself, and he responds to Frank Churchill's proposal to undertake the journey with trepidation: 'there are a great many houses; you might be very much at a loss, and it is a very dirty walk, unless you keep on the foot-path' (195). Similarly, a winter visit to Randalls is looked upon as 'a very great event' (108), and the strawberry-picking expedition marks Mr Woodhouse's first visit to Donwell in two years. Yet the houses are only half a mile and one mile respectively from Hartfield.[4] More significant upheavals, like the marriages and consequent removals from Hartfield of Isabella and Miss Taylor, almost completely disorient Mr Woodhouse.

Although he does not go to such comic extremes, Mr Knightley, the other leader of the Highbury community, is also in danger of becoming too content with his present situation.[5] At the age of thirty-seven, he is already a confirmed bachelor, and while others engage in the courtship ritual of the dance, he prefers to stand among 'the bulky forms and stooping shoulders of the elderly men' (326). Changes in the familiar routine are as unpleasant to Mr Knightley as to Mr Woodhouse, and he expresses distaste for the

idea of reviving the long-lapsed custom of balls at the Crown: 'Oh!
yes, I must be there; I could not refuse; and I will keep as much
awake as I can; but I would rather be at home, looking over William
Larkins's week's account' (257).

The efforts of these two enemies of change are aided on occasion
by Mr John Knightley, who is no less unfriendly to breaks in his
routine. The Westons' party, for example, involves a disruption of
the family group to which he is accustomed at Christmas, and he
complains vehemently about having to attend: 'It is the greatest
absurdity—Actually snowing at this moment!—The folly of not
allowing people to be comfortable at home' (113). John Knightley's
objections to socialising, however, run rather deeper than his
brother's or Mr Woodhouse's, for whereas they see it as a nuisance,
he regards it as a positive evil. For him, anything that takes the
individual outside the home necessarily weakens the all-important
domestic virtues. He is very critical, for example, of Mr Weston's
love of company:

> Mr Weston is rather an easy, cheerful tempered man, than a man
> of strong feelings; he takes things as he finds them, and makes
> enjoyment of them somehow or other, depending, I suspect,
> much more upon what is called *society* for his comforts, that is,
> upon the power of eating and drinking, and playing whist with
> his neighbours five times a-week, than upon family affection, or
> any thing that home affords.   (96)

Similarly, it requires only the slightest increase in Emma's social life
before John Knightley begins to suggest that she may no longer
have time for her nephews: 'I hope I am aware that they . . . may
be some incumbrance to you, if your visiting-engagements continue
to increase as much as they have done lately' (311).

· The person who suffers most from the excessive conservatism of
Highbury society is Emma Woodhouse. There is a sameness to the
daily round of events in the village which inevitably makes life
extremely boring for anyone possessing the vitality of youth. The
novel's opening sentence, which asserts that Emma· 'had lived
nearly twenty-one years in the world with very little to distress or
vex her' (5), is usually taken simply as the introduction to Jane
Austen's indictment of a character that has become selfish through
over-indulgence. However, it also constitutes a poignant summary
of the emptiness of the first twenty-one years of Emma's life. And,

indeed, the novel's opening pages are full of suggestions about the lack of genuine stimulation in Emma's environment. The completion of Miss Taylor's wedding, for example, leaves Emma and her father 'to dine together, with no prospect of a third to cheer a long evening' (6). Neither is there anything more enlivening to look forward to than 'the common course of Hartfield days' (262) in the months to come: 'many a long October and November evening must be struggled through at Hartfield, before Christmas brought the next visit from Isabella and her husband and their little children to fill the house and give her pleasant society again' (7). What social life the Woodhouses do have is shaped entirely according to Mr Woodhouse's interests, and there is little to entertain Emma in the company of elderly ladies like Mrs Goddard and Mrs and Miss Bates: 'the quiet prosings of three such women made her feel that every evening so spent, was indeed one of the long evenings she had fearfully anticipated' (22). Even straying beyond the confines of Hartfield and into the village which Mr Woodhouse finds so dangerous is not very rewarding because 'much could not be hoped from the traffic of even the busiest part of Highbury' (233).

The way in which life is organised in Highbury not only makes things dull for Emma, it also deprives her of opportunities to achieve personal growth. Formal social gatherings may seem irrelevant to someone like Mr Woodhouse, whose life has passed through all its important transitions apart from death, but in fact their absence guarantees that Emma remains a child. Her manners and morals will not mature without the testing and correction that only exposure to the strict codes of behaviour that operate in the formal context can offer; and the marriage that defines a woman's adult role will be denied her unless she is allowed to engage in courtship rituals. The limiting effect of this lack of formal social life is nowhere more evident than in Emma's relationship with Mr Knightley. The frequent casual visits of this intellectually vigorous and morally demanding man provide Emma with some of the stimulation she generally lacks. Nevertheless, their relationship is an unsatisfactory one because, like so many things in Highbury, it has become static. The basic pattern of intercourse between Emma and Mr Knightley was established when Emma was a child and, since it has not changed in the intervening years, it is hardly surprising that neither is able to contemplate the other as a possible lover. Only by coming together in a context appropriate for courtship, such as dancing, can Emma and Mr Knightley hope to recognise that the affection that exists between them could be better expressed through a new kind of intimacy.

Yet, for all the deprivations she suffers under the Highbury regime, Emma is not interested in changing her way of life. It is true that she joins Frank Churchill in promoting the Crown ball, and is eager to take part in the trips to Donwell and Box Hill. However, she is interested in these social rituals only for the temporary amusement they can afford her, and does not begin to recognise their significance as agents of change. She is content, for example, to open the Crown ball with Frank Churchill, even though she has long discounted him as a possible suitor. Emma's conservatism derives in part from an awareness that Highbury society as it is possesses many admirable qualities. The attentions she pays her father and the respect she reveals for John Knightley's love of the family circle show, for example, that Emma is firmly attached to her society's ideal of domesticity. And the dignified opposition she offers to the vulgar Mrs Elton demonstrates an equally thorough acceptance of its gentlemanly values of politeness and respect for others. Emma's conservatism also owes something to a suspicion of the consequences of change that she has doubtless inherited from her father. Thus, although Emma is much more generous in her reponse to Miss Taylor's marriage than Mr Woodhouse, neverthe-less, in so far as it alters her own situation, she can see it only as a bad thing: 'The event had every promise of happiness for her friend . . . but it was a black morning's work for her. The want of Miss Taylor would be felt every hour of every day' (6). The confidence with which Emma is able to tell Harriet that she will never marry is also based to a much greater extent than she would be ready to admit in simple fear of change: 'I must see somebody very superior to any one I have seen yet, to be tempted . . . I would rather not be tempted. I cannot really change for the better' (84). Even less admirable than this are Emma's snobbish reasons for wanting to keep things as they are. Emma moves within a very small circle which is bounded by the three houses of Hartfield, Donwell and Randalls, and she is of great, indeed, first importance in each. Change means admitting others into this circle, and she might not be so highly regarded by these others. Thus, Emma is hostile to the Coles' very proper social ambitions, and is horrified at the possibility that Mr Knightley might marry. The exclusiveness of her world is so important to Emma that if she had her way she would narrow it still further. The Bates' family, for instance, although an object of great concern to Mr Woodhouse and Mr Knightley, has little appeal for her. This is partly because she objects to Miss Bates' prattling, and to the low company she and her mother keep. However, it is also because she usually finds that when they are present talk of the highly accomplished and elegant Jane Fairfax inevitably offers a temporary challenge to her own social supremacy. Only by reminding herself of her duties as a member of Highbury society is Emma able to pay the Bateses even a semblance of the attention owed to them (156).

Emma, then, has very strong reasons for disliking change. Nevertheless, we would expect that the sheer boredom of living in a world which does not offer her any legitimate grounds upon which to act would inevitably force her to attempt to establish a more dynamic relationship with her community. This does not turn out to be the case, however, because, as an 'imaginist' (335), Emma is able to re-direct her energies into the creation of an extremely entertaining private world which she populates with people who, because they come from beyond Highbury, she believes lie outside her sphere of responsible behaviour. In this world Harriet Smith becomes a gentleman's daughter, Frank Churchill an ideal young man, and Jane Fairfax a loose woman. Emma is, of course, completely unjustified in assuming that, simply because she lacks personal experience of their origins, these people are undefined and shapeless objects that can be forced into any mould she thinks appropriate. There may be some mystery surrounding Harriet's birth. Nevertheless her present situation yields enough evidence to make attempts at defining her 'proper subordination' more than a matter of 'fancy' (180). Mr Knightley, for instance, has very little trouble in arriving at a precise assessment of Harriet's social position vis à vis her two potential husbands:

> What are Harriet Smith's claims, either of birth, nature or education, to any connection higher than Robert Martin? She is the natural daughter of nobody knows whom, with probably no settled provision at all, and certainly no respectable relations. She is known only as parlour-boarder at a common school.   (61)

> Depend upon it, Elton will not do. Elton is a very good sort of man, and a very respectable vicar of Highbury, but not at all likely to make an imprudent match. He knows the value of a good income as well as anybody.   (66)

Similarly, although Jane Fairfax is extremely reserved about her odd decision to spend so long in Highbury rather than visit Ireland with the Campbells, there is enough evidence in the looks Mr Knightley observes her exchanging with Frank Churchill of her real motives to make nonsense of Emma's arbitrary assumption that she is fleeing an emotional entanglement with Mr Dixon (343–4). Neither does the fact that Frank Churchill has never visited Highbury leave him sufficiently unknown for Emma to be free to characterise him as a potential 'treasure at Highbury', a man who will cause a *'sensation'* (149) and revitalise the community:

> My idea of him is, that he can adapt his conversation to the taste of every body, and has the power as well as the wish of being universally agreeable. To you, he will talk of farming; to me, of drawing or music; and so on to every body.   (150)

The style of his letters and his failure to pay Mr Weston's new wife the respect of an early visit make it much more likely, as Mr Knightley points out, that, far from being the symbol of perfection Emma imagines, Frank Churchill is 'proud, luxurious, and selfish' (145), 'a very weak young man' (148), with 'nothing really amiable about him' (149).

A comparison of Emma's conversations with Mrs Weston and Mr Knightley about Frank Churchill makes it clear that these misjudgements result from wilfulness rather than lack of intelligence. The assessment of Frank that Emma offers Mrs Weston is for once based on the evidence available, and turns out to be almost identical to that which Mr Knightley makes later. Thus Emma says: 'He ought to come . . . If he could stay only a couple of days, he ought to come; and one can hardly conceive a young man's not having it in his power to do as much as that' (122). And Mr Knightley: 'I cannot believe that he has not the power of coming, if he made a point of it . . . It is not to be conceived that a man of three or four-and-twenty should not have liberty of mind or limb to that amount' (145–6). The first words are Emma's; the second Mr Knightley's. But in this instance they are completely interchangeable. Nevertheless, Emma responds to Mr Knightley's analysis of Frank Churchill by telling him that he is 'the worst judge in the world' (146). This is because it is not in her interests to accept the very common sense which was her own shortly before. Highbury is dull and predictable, but can be tolerated so long as the outside world is made to appear romantic and exciting. Once it becomes accommodated within an overall logical framework and is thus made equally predictable, as Mr Knightley suggests it should be,[6] it will no longer serve as a source of escape for Emma. Then, she will be forced to look within her own community for stimulation, a search which will inevitably force her to instigate the change which she fears so much.[7]

The nature, the limitations and the consequences of Emma's failure to adopt a consistent approach to all aspects of her experience are revealed very clearly by the seven formal social occasions around which the novel is organised.[8] The last three also mark out the main stages in the process by which, in spite of herself, she achieves an integrated vision and the maturity to participate in necessary change. The central problem of character with which Jane Austen is concerned in *Emma* is established by the contrast between her heroine's behaviour during parties at Hartfield and Randalls, and during the main action of the first volume. Throughout her attempts to make a match between Harriet and Mr Elton, both of whom originate from beyond the boundaries of Highbury, Emma acts with a complete disregard for the feelings of others or for social realities. Yet, at the Hartfield and Randalls parties, both of which are very much Highbury affairs, she is inspired by respect for her community to conduct herself with propriety and displays an acute concern for the needs of her companions. This contrast is further developed in the second section of *Emma*, which is organised around two parties. During the party given by the Coles, people she considers outsiders, Emma again behaves unfeelingly and yields herself up to her fantasies. At Hartfield, however, Emma upholds the very best of Highbury standards against the challenge offered by the bourgeois Mrs Elton. A delicate balance between reality and fantasy, dullness and excitement, responsibility and irresponsibility, is thus established, and by this means Emma holds her world in a condition of stasis.

However, the balance begins to tip during the Crown ball and the Donwell visit. There are two factors which upset it. First, both occasions are part of the revival of Highbury social life inspired by Frank Churchill and Mrs Elton and, being much more exciting than the familiar evening parties at Hartfield and Randalls, they command Emma's complete involvement. Mr Knightley, too, is shaken out of his usual complacency and participates fully. As a result, and without either being aware of it, Mr Knightley and

Emma begin to precipitate change by approaching each other as lovers. Second, areas of experience in which Emma had felt herself free from normal moral and social restrictions begin to impinge on those in which she has always acknowledged the need to act responsibly. Thus, a discordant note is introduced into both the Crown ball and the Donwell visit by hints that, because of Emma's interference with her sense of rank, Harriet has become presumptuous enough to aspire to be Mrs Knightley. The harmony of the Donwell visit is further undercut by the evident distress of Frank Churchill and Jane Fairfax, whose already unstable relationship has been brought to an impasse by their involvement in Emma's fantasies.

Emma does not achieve a complete understanding of the limitations she imposes on herself by her failure to adopt a consistent approach to experience until she learns of Harriet's ambitions regarding Mr Knightley and of Frank Churchill's engagement to Jane Fairfax. However, the essential truth is revealed to her during the novel's last major formal social occasion, the excursion to Box Hill. There, perhaps inspired by travelling completely beyond the bounds of Highbury for the only time in the novel, Emma gives in momentarily to her long-standing wish to treat Miss Bates with the kind of disregard for propriety and humanity that she usually reserves for outsiders. This lapse, the implications of which Mr Knightley quickly points out to her, is enough to make Emma see that her world cannot be divided up into two separate compartments conveniently sealed off from each other. Her task from that point on, and it is one that becomes increasingly more evident with the mortifying revelations about Harriet, Frank Churchill and Jane Fairfax that follow in rapid succession, is to direct her energies inward towards her own community, and to seek stimulation in a generous engagement with the familiar and in a readiness to accept change. Thus, Emma at last pays proper attention to Miss Bates, seeks to be of use to Jane Fairfax, and yields gladly to the alteration in her own status and the order of village life consequent on accepting Mr Knightley's marriage proposal.

Harriet Smith's role in the opening section of the novel is established by her first meeting with Emma. An evening spent with Mr Woodhouse, Mrs Goddard, Mrs and Miss Bates promises Emma no more satisfaction than that which can be gained from doing her duty towards her father. However, because of Harriet's inclusion in the party, the occasion turns out to be much more entertaining than anticipated. Harriet herself is not responsible for this improvement because, apart from physical beauty, there is little that is especially pleasing about her. Rather, it results from what Emma's imagination is able to make out of her interesting situation. The mystery surrounding Harriet's birth and the unformed quality of her character free Emma from the limitations that must normally surround speculation about another person's future prospects. Consequently, she is able to spend much of the evening within the confines of her imagination, and is spared most of the tedium she anticipated. This temporary escape proves very beneficial to Emma in that, when her attention is finally recalled to her father, she is able to meet his needs with a readiness that might not otherwise have been achieved quite so easily:

> She was so busy in admiring those soft blue eyes, in talking and listening, and forming all these schemes in the in-betweens, that the evening flew away at a very unusual rate; and the supper-table, which always closed such parties, and for which she had been used to sit and watch the due time, was all set out and ready, and moved forwards to the fire, before she was aware. With an alacrity beyond the common impulse of a spirit which yet was never indifferent to the credit of doing every thing well and attentively, with the real good-will of a mind delighted with its own ideas, did she then do all the honours of the meal.   (24)

In order that Harriet might continue to function as the leading character in a world created entirely by Emma's own imagination, the latter is forced to ignore the realities of birth and rank and to operate instead according to a system of subordination by fancy. Mr Knightley's inconvenient comments about Harriet's social position must be discounted; Robert Martin, a suitor appropriate to Harriet's real situation in life, must be rejected; and the ambitious and calculating Mr Elton must be transformed into a romantic lover. Only Mr Elton makes self-deceit easy for Emma, since his style as a suitor (unfortunately, as it turns out, of Emma rather than Harriet) is based on the conventions of romance. He responds to Emma's portrait of Harriet with 'raptures' (43), 'he does sigh and languish' (49), and he composes an elegant charade on courtship. It is therefore a simple task for Emma to fit Mr Elton into the role she had planned for him.

Mr Knightley is rather more difficult to deal with because Emma had 'a sort of habitual respect for his judgment in general' (65), and yet to accept what he says about Harriet, Robert Martin and Mr Elton would completely destroy her fantasy world. The fact that Emma is able to convince herself that Mr Knightley can be ignored pays testimony to the strength of her conviction that the standards of Highbury do not apply when dealing with outsiders. Mr Knightley may well have been almost always right over a lifetime of encounters in their own community, but this, for Emma, does not mean that he knows anything about a world based on delicate (and, indeed, imagined) points of 'female right and refinement' (65) and on 'strong passion' (67). Consequently, although it troubles Emma to disagree with him, she has no doubt that it is correct to do so.

The rejection of Robert Martin's claims involves Emma in a particularly perverse manipulation of rank since, in actual fact, Harriet would do very well to marry a young man who has enough money not to be troubled by her lack of wealth and is of sufficiently low status not to be over-concerned about her illegitimacy. As a yeoman, Robert Martin occupies a very respectable position within English society, and one that is much admired by Mr Knightley. Emma, however, manages to belittle it by persistently gauging Robert Martin's manners against standards more applicable to the gentry.[9] When Harriet, for instance, becomes too enthusiastic about the extremely kind attentions Robert Martin has paid to Mrs Goddard, Emma tries to remove the favourable impression that he has created by enquiring sourly about the extent of his reading (28–9). Similarly, Emma reduces Robert Martin's perfectly proper performance during a chance meeting with Harriet on the Donwell road to the 'clownish' (32) by comparing him with the most refined members of Highbury society:

I think, Harriet, since your acquaintance with us, you have been repeatedly in the company of some, such very real gentleman, that you must yourself be struck with the difference in Mr Martin. At Hartfield you have had very good specimens of well educated, well bred men. I should be surprized if, after seeing them, you could be in company with Mr Martin again without perceiving him to be a very inferior creature.   (32–3)

However, such displays of self-deceit, wilful ignorance of social realities, and irreponsible and selfish manipulation of others do not give us a full picture of Emma, because she reserves them for her dealings with Harriet and Mr Elton, neither of whom has his origins within Highbury. On the two occasions during and, indeed as I am suggesting partly because of, her involvement in the Elton–Harriet affair, when Emma meets formally with the inner circle of her own community, she displays a keen sense of the needs of others and good judgement. During the social evening at Hartfield which is organised to greet the John Knightleys, Mr Woodhouse is at his most tiresome, and persists in bringing up his obsessions about health and travel. There is much in the occasion, then, to try the patience of anyone, let alone a young woman of overflowing energy and imagination, and John Knightley, in fact, several times comes close to losing his temper. Emma, however, who is finding more than enough stimulation in trying to arrange Harriet's future, behaves impeccably throughout. Even before the party begins, she displays a 'consideration of what was due to each brother' (98) by ensuring that Mr Knightley is invited to meet John. To do this she has to overcome Mr Woodhouse's wish to keep Isabella to himself on her first day at Hartfield. A similar concern with the needs of others characterises her two interventions in the conversation of the guests. First, when she sees that her father is upsetting himself over the question of sea air, Emma steps in and diverts him away from the 'unsafe subject' (101). And second, she changes the topic of conversation in order to prevent a squabble that Mr Woodhouse has engendered between Isabella and John Knightley from developing:

> 'My dear Isabella,'—exclaimed he hastily—'pray do not concern yourself about my looks. Be satisfied with doctoring and coddling yourself and the children, and let me look as I chuse.'
> 'I did not thoroughly understand what you were telling your brother,' cried Emma, 'about your friend Mr Graham's intending to have a bailiff from Scotland, to look after his new estate.'   (104)

In her conduct on this occasion Emma resembles no one more than that very same Mr Knightley with whom she is at such odds over Harriet, for he too takes the needs of others as his first responsibility. Thus, when Emma is unable to stop Mr Woodhouse from pursuing a subject that is obviously annoying John Knightley, Mr Knightley comes to her rescue by distracting his brother's attention:

'True, true,' cried Mr Knightley, with most ready inter-
position—'very true. That's a consideration indeed.—But John,
as to what I was telling you of my idea of moving the path to
Langham, of turning it more to the right that it may not cut
through the home meadows, I cannot conceive any
difficulty.'   (106)

At the Westons' party, too, which is limited to 'their own especial
set' (108), Emma's conduct is irreproachable. On the journey there
she does what little she can to improve John Knightley's temper by
suppressing the temptation to quarrel with him, and during the
evening she puts the group ahead of the self by eschewing a *tête-à-tête*
with Mrs Weston, even though it might have yielded more
information on the interesting subject of Frank Churchill. It is the
affair of the snowstorm, however, which truly justifies Jane Austen's
claim that Emma has just the right feelings for Mr Weston's party:
'Mr Elton must smile less, and Mr John Knightley more, to fit them
for the place.—Emma only might be as nature prompted' (117). Mr
Weston, who conceals his knowledge of the inclement weather in
order that his party might not be broken up early, and John
Knightley, who maliciously exaggerates the violence of the storm,
are both neglectful of their duty to Mr Woodhouse. Emma,
however, makes him the first object of her attention and strives to
allay his childish fears: 'To her he looked for comfort; and her
assurances of safety, her representation of the excellence of the
horses, and of James, and of their having so many friends about
them, revived him a little' (126–7). Again, when she acts responsibly Emma begins to resemble Mr Knightley, because he too
acknowledges the importance of meeting Mr Woodhouse's needs.
The close understanding that Emma and Mr Knightley achieve on
such occasions is epitomised by the manner in which they instantly
concur in what action should be taken after it becomes clear that
nothing will reconcile Mr Woodhouse to staying at the party:

While the others were variously urging and recommending, Mr
Knightley and Emma settled it in a few brief sentences: thus—
    'Your father will not be easy; why do not you go?'
    'I am ready, if the others are.'
    'Shall I ring the bell?'
    'Yes, do.'   (128)

The events of the carriage ride home, when Mr Elton reveals that he is really interested in making a profitable match with the wealthy heiress rather than a romantic one with her penniless friend, suggest to the reader that there is no guarantee that Emma will be able to keep the two parts into which she has divided her world separate. Emma herself, however, although mortified by her mistakes, is too committed to her perverse approach to experience to acknowledge its limitations. Thus, as a comparison of her conduct during dinner parties at the Coles' and at Hartfield reveals, she continues to behave with similar inconsistency during the second section of the novel. The Coles have lived respectably in Highbury for a number of years, and both Mr Woodhouse and Mr Knightley acknowledge the justice of their claims to stand on an equal footing with the best families. Emma, however, regards them as outsiders because they are relative newcomers and their background is in trade. Therefore, her initial reaction to the invitation she receives to dine at their house is to reject it: 'The Coles were very respectable in their way, but they ought to be taught that it was not for them to arrange the terms on which the superior families would visit them' (207). Later, she changes her mind, but this owes nothing to any reassessment of the Coles' relationship to the Highbury community. Before the party, Emma resolves 'to be very happy, in spite of the scene being laid at Mr Cole's' (213), and in retrospect she decides that she 'did not repent her condescension in going to the Coles' (231). Both comments are indicative of a continued refusal to grant the Coles the respect due to them, and in fact Emma goes to their party only because she realises that it will provide her with opportunities to continue her interesting new relationship with Frank Churchill.

Emma's preconceptions about what is permissible in the company of 'outsiders' like the Coles are so strong that she is completely uninfluenced by the acute concern with propriety that characterises all aspects of the proceedings. In their invitation to the Hartfield family, the Coles, as Emma admits herself, 'expressed themselves so properly—there was so much real attention in the manner of it—so much consideration for her father' (208). The guest-list is irreproachable, since, in addition to Emma's own circle, it includes only a 'proper unobjectionable country family' (214) and Mr Cox, the Highbury lawyer. The dinner itself, during which 'every corner dish was placed exactly right' (218) is a model of correctness. And the lesser worthies make their entry after dinner very properly 'in their different divisions' (219). None of this attention to correct form, however, can divert Emma from her irresponsible and self-indulgent goals. She is equally impervious to the good example set by Mr Knightley who, by thinking to provide a carriage for the Bateses, and by preventing Frank Churchill from forcing a tired Jane Fairfax into further singing, provides cogent reminders of what the individual owes to his fellows.

At dinner, then, Emma clearly feels herself to be under no obligation to further the harmony of the group, and disengages herself from Frank Churchill only when forced to do so: 'The conversation was here interrupted. They were called on to share in the awkwardness of a rather long interval between the courses, and obliged to be as formal and as orderly as the others' (218). Even while temporarily separated from Frank Churchill, after she retires with the ladies into the drawing room, Emma makes no attempt to involve herself with the other guests: 'To be in company, nicely dressed herself and seeing others nicely dressed, to sit and smile and look pretty, and say nothing, was enough for the happiness of the present hour' (219). And when Frank rejoins the ladies, they quickly renew their *tête-à-tête*: 'after paying his compliments en passant to Miss Bates and her niece, [Frank] made his way directly to the opposite side of the circle, where sat Miss Woodhouse; and till he could find a seat by her, would not sit at all' (220). The content of their private conversation compounds its basic impropriety because Emma, whose 'fancy' has received 'an amusing supply' (214) from the mysterious story of Jane Fairfax's piano, allows herself to be egged on by Frank Churchill into voicing scandalous and ground-less suspicions about Jane's relationship with Mr Dixon:

> I do not mean to reflect upon the good intentions of either Mr
> Dixon or Miss Fairfax, but I cannot help suspecting either that,
> after making his proposals to her friend, he had the misfortune to
> fall in love with *her*, or that he became conscious of a little
> attachment on her side.   (217)

Emma approaches the Hartfield dinner party in a very different spirit. As we saw earlier, the home setting is always enough to inspire a sense of responsibility in her. On this occasion, however, she is particularly attentive to her social duty because she is acutely aware that the guest of honour, Mrs Elton, offers a threat to the Highbury ideal of order and propriety. Emma's concern that everything be right is very evident in her attitude to the guest list. The possibility of an awkward meeting between Harriet and Mr Elton, for example, causes her considerable anxiety. And, when freed from this worry by Harriet's tactful refusal of her invitation, Emma seeks to further the propriety of the occasion by replacing her with Jane Fairfax, thus correcting her long-standing negligence of a person she knows she should value for her links with Highbury: 'I ought to have been more her friend.—She will never like me now. I have neglected her too long. But I will shew her greater attention than I have done' (291). Emma also reacts in a serious and responsible way to the further alterations in the guest list that result from John Knightley's unexpected arrival and Mr Weston's enforced absence. Glad as she would be herself to have John Knightley's company, Emma regrets this increase in the party because it offers a threat to the comfort of Mr Woodhouse who 'considered eight persons at dinner together as the utmost that his nerves could bear' (292). Similarly, although she personally laments the loss of Mr Weston, Emma's main reaction is one of relief that the party is again of a size to suit Mr Woodhouse: 'Mr Weston was unexpectedly summoned to town and must be absent on the very day . . . Mr Woodhouse was quite at ease; and the seeing him so . . . removed the chief of even Emma's vexations' (292). The needs of others continue to guide Emma during the evening itself. She remains true, for example, to her resolution to treat Jane Fairfax as a member of the Bates' family, rather than as Colonel Campbell's ward, an outsider towards whom she has no responsibilities, and manages to restrain herself even when granted an excellent opportunity to pass a remark about Mr Dixon:

> She could have made an inquiry or two, as to the expedition and the expense of the Irish mails;—it was at her tongue's end—but she abstained. She was quite determined not to utter a word that should hurt Jane Fairfax's feelings.   (298)

In many ways, Emma's attempts to ensure the success of the evening are fruitful. Mr Woodhouse is so happily occupied in making 'every fair lady welcome and easy' (295) that not even the news that Jane Fairfax has been out in the rain can disturb his tranquillity; John Knightley displays none of the irritation that might have been expected of him at being forced to take part in a large party, but rather occupies himself in a pleasant conversation with Jane Fairfax; Mr Knightley is pleased enough at Emma's conduct to be willing to engage her in a bantering conversation about her increased social life; and Mrs Weston behaves in her usual considerate and friendly manner. However, although Mrs Elton is not allowed to take control of the proceedings, she manages to be a disruptive force throughout, and at times seriously challenges Emma's attempts to preserve the unity of the group:

> When the ladies returned to the drawing-room after dinner, Emma found it hardly possible to prevent their making two distinct parties;—with so much perseverance in judging and behaving ill did Mrs Elton engross Jane Fairfax and slight herself.   (299)

A contrast is thus established in which Mrs Elton's vulgarity, pretentiousness and outright rudeness do much to point up the excellence of Emma's behaviour. However, what is perhaps even more significant, a number of parallels are also drawn between Mrs Elton's conduct at Hartfield and Emma's at the Coles' and during her attempts to match Harriet and Mr Elton, which very firmly establish just how far Emma strays away from acceptable standards in her dealings with outsiders.[10]

Mrs Elton makes herself particularly objectionable during her conversations with Jane Fairfax. Early in the evening, Mrs Weston and John Knightley are content simply to express their concern with Jane's health after it emerges that she was caught in the rain during her daily visit to the post office. Mrs Elton, however, persists in making unwanted offers of help, and becomes so caught up in displaying her bounteous nature and boasting of the superfluity of her servants that she completely fails to notice that she is causing acute distress to the object of her attentions (295–6). Later, a desire to demonstrate her wealth of influential contacts makes Mrs Elton press Jane on the obviously unwelcome subject of her future employment (299–302). A similar lack of respect for the unique existence of others lies at the root of Emma's assumption that she has a right to cast doubts on Jane Fairfax's morals, to distort Frank Churchill's character, and to manipulate Harriet Smith's rank simply to provide herself with a source of entertainment. Mrs Elton is also like Emma in that each has an excessive sense of her own importance. Mrs Elton, for example, assumes automatically that she will lead the way into dinner:

> before Mr Woodhouse had reached her with his request to be

allowed to hand her into the dining-parlour, [Mrs Elton] was saying—

> 'Must I go first? I really am ashamed of always leading the way.'   (298)

And Emma sees it as only natural that she be the first to play at the Coles: 'and as, in every respect, it suited Emma best to lead, she gave a very proper compliance' (227). In both cases, this sense of superiority derives from a failure to grant sufficient importance to things that fall outside their own little worlds. Emma is unable to see anything beyond the confines of Hartfield, Donwell and Randalls, and Mrs Elton, as Mr Weston finds to his chagrin, judges everything in terms of Maple Grove:

> 'Indeed!—from Yorkshire I think. Enscombe is in Yorkshire?'
> 'Yes, they are about 190 miles from London. A considerable journey.'
> 'Yes, upon my word, very considerable. Sixty-five miles farther than from Maple Grove to London . . .'
> '[Enscombe] is a retired place. A fine place, but very retired.'
> 'Aye—like Maple Grove, I dare say.'   (305–7)

Furthermore, although Emma is quite justifiably offended by the rude way in which Mrs Elton divides up her party by annexing Jane Fairfax's attention, her own behaviour at the Coles', where she consistently separates herself and Frank Churchill from the group, is no better.

Emma's fragmented approach to experience, then, not only blinds her to the need for changes in her relationship to Highbury society, it also at times reduces her to the moral level of a Mrs Elton. Clearly the pattern of behaviour in which Emma has become caught up must be broken, and the process which brings her to an awareness of this need is set in motion by the Crown ball. Although balls were once a familiar feature of Highbury social life, the custom has been in abeyance for such a long time that the community regards Emma and Frank Churchill's plan to open up the Crown for dancing as a rather startling innovation, and raises a number of objections to it. Mr Woodhouse dislikes the idea because the room at the Crown falls beyond his tiny area of knowledge, and because he assumes it will be damp and draughty; Mr Knightley takes exception because a ball

would disturb his well-regulated routine; Mrs Weston emphasises
the dirty condition of the room and the lack of supper facilities; and
even Emma's desire for novelty is briefly halted by doubts about the
'confusion of rank' (198) that must be tolerated if enough couples
are to be found. There is, of course, nothing improper about a ball,
especially when it is arranged, as on this occasion, with keen
attention to 'the rights of men and women' (254). Nevertheless, Mr
Woodhouse and his friends are not entirely unjustified in feeling
threatened by it. Social life in Highbury up to this point has been
regulated to a pace and level of energy that suits Mr Woodhouse,
and has therefore placed such an overwhelming emphasis on the
familiar as to become almost static and extremely soporific.
Dancing, however, while it operates within confined and well-
regulated limits, is an activity which allows movement and scope for
choosing and changing partners.[11] As such it encourages a much
more open and dynamic society than that over which Mr
Woodhouse presides, and it is significant that while his needs are not
ignored on this occasion, they cannot be met within the framework
of the ball itself. Thus, while the community as a whole gathers at
the Crown, Mr Woodhouse is left safe at home to enjoy 'a vast deal
of chat, and backgammon' (329) with Mrs Bates.

   This at last, then, is a Highbury social occasion that not only
places a burden of responsibility on Emma, but also provides her
with opportunities to engage in activities appropriate to her age and
situation. As a result she discovers that proper behaviour can satisfy
her need for stimulation, and she begins to develop a more
satisfactory relationship with her community. This is not to say that
Emma is conscious of the process in which she is becoming involved,
for indeed she has little sense of the ball's significance as a courtship
ritual and agent of change. Her willingness to accept as her first
partner Frank Churchill, whom she has already decided she will
never marry, makes this obvious. The process is no less real for all
that, as is revealed by the fact that her attitude towards Mr
Knightley undergoes a remarkable transformation in the course of
the evening. Immediately prior to the ball, Emma is as blind as ever
to the possibility that Mr Knightley's role in her life might ever
change. Therefore, even though she offers a definition of her ideal
man that fits Mr Knightley perfectly, it never occurs to her for a
moment that a suitable lover is so close at hand: 'General
benevolence, but not general friendship, made a man what he ought
to be.—She could fancy such a man' (320). Awareness begins to

dawn during the ball itself, however. Previous Highbury social occasions have been so safe and predictable that, apart from occasionally demonstrating his kindness and consideration, Mr Knightley has been called on to do little to ensure the preservation of harmony. Therefore, as in his refusal to dance at the Coles', he has assumed a background role consistent with his image of himself as a confirmed bachelor. However, more active displays of virtue are necessary if propriety is to withstand the strains imposed on it by the open and flexible style of the Crown ball. One incident in particular illustrates this. Harriet Smith, who was able to provide against meeting Mr Elton at Hartfield, is inevitably brought face to face with him on this occasion by the permutations of pairing involved in the choosing of partners. Since Mr Elton uses the encounter to take revenge for the offence that Harriet has unintentionally done him, and gives a public demonstration of his unwillingness to dance with her, a situation is created that causes Harriet pain and embarrassment and offers a challenge to the propriety of the whole occasion. To lurk amongst the 'husbands, and fathers, and whist-players' (325) is no longer good enough, and Mr Knightley must now come forward and rescue Harriet by engaging her himself. This display of polite heroism, and the position into which it forces him amongst the young and eligible, where his performance is 'extremely good' (328), has a profound effect on Emma's view of Mr Knightley. Thus, she does not find it strange that when they next meet he asks her to dance, and indeed replies in such a way as to indicate that she is on the verge of viewing him as a suitor:

'Will you?' said he, offering his hand.
'Indeed I will. You have shown that you can dance, and you know we are not really so much brother and sister as to make it at all improper.'   (331)

The visit to Donwell marks a further stage in Emma's reassessment of her role in the Highbury community. Like balls at the Crown, excursions to Donwell are not a part of the normal pattern of Highbury life. Mr Woodhouse has not been there for two years, and even the more energetic Emma has been absent for long enough to be 'eager to refresh and correct her memory' (357-8). Thus, although the gathering of a few friends to pick strawberries and eat lunch cannot match a ball for excitement, the mere fact that it does happen is an important sign that Highbury is becoming less set in its ways. Indeed, in at least one sense, the visit augurs even better than the ball for the future of the village because it offers clear evidence that Mr Knightley is prepared to take on fully the active moral role that he played briefly at the Crown.

Whereas he was most unwilling to participate in the ball, Mr Knightley now becomes an initiator of social activity. Mrs Elton's reaction to the cancellation of her visit to Box Hill makes it obvious to Mr Knightley that she is likely to come up with an extremely improper scheme by way of compensation. To avoid this he offers her an alternative form of amusement in the shape of a strawberry-picking party in the grounds of his house, thereby ensuring that her restless energies will be placed under his personal control. The success of Mr Knightley's manoeuvre is evident in the prompt and firm way he is able to check Mrs Elton's attempts to be 'Lady Patroness' (354):

'It is my party. Leave it all to me. I will invite your guests.'

'No,'—he calmly replied,—'There is but one married woman in the world whom I can ever allow to invite what guests she pleases to Donwell, and that one is . . . Mrs Knightley;—and, till she is in being, I will manage such matters myself.' (354–5)

Mr Knightley's capacities as a host, however, are far from exhausted by the task of keeping Mrs Elton in her place, and he ensures that the entire visit is organised in such a way as to reflect the very best standards. Mr Woodhouse's comfort is, of course, the first object of his concern. Therefore, Mrs Elton's proposal of a picnic lunch is rejected because sitting out of doors would make the old man ill, and none of the guests is allowed to embark on the picking of strawberries until Mr Woodhouse is comfortably settled in front of the fire. Once propriety has been attended to, Mr Knightley engages himself in the other function of a responsible citizen, that of effecting necessary change. As the guests scatter over his grounds, Mr Knightley attaches himself to Harriet and takes her to a spot overlooking Abbey Mill Farm. His intention is to remind her of the 'prosperity and beauty' (360) of Robert Martin's home environment, and thus to direct her attentions back to a most proper suitor.

Emma is greatly enlivened by this further example of energetic social activity, and commits herself totally to the occasion, which she approaches with 'very high expectations of pleasure' (357). Much of her behaviour is of course what we would expect from her during any activity in which she is concerned to keep to Highbury rules. Mr Woodhouse naturally occupies a good deal of her attention, and she shares with Mrs Weston the task of keeping him amused; Jane Fairfax evokes in her the kind of genuine concern she felt earlier at Hartfield; and Frank Churchill is treated as a fractious guest who must be soothed, rather than as an object of fantasy. The main focus of Emma's day, however, is the revitalised Mr Knightley and his estate. Viewed within the context of his own home Mr Knightley is indeed an impressive figure, and Emma finds herself feeling an increasing respect for him:

> She felt all the honest pride and complacency which her alliance with the present and future proprietor could fairly warrant, as she viewed the respectable size and style of the building, its suitable, becoming, characteristic situation, low and sheltered—its ample gardens stretching down to meadows washed by a stream, of which the Abbey, with all the old neglect of prospect, had scarcely a sight—and its abundance of timber in rows and avenues which neither fashion nor extravagance had rooted up.

Her conclusion that all this 'was just what it ought to be, and . . . looked what it was' makes it clear that Emma is tending towards a rather more direct 'alliance with the present . . . proprietor' (358) than is already afforded by her sister's marriage, and that she is beginning to realise that there is an appropriate role for her amongst such a fine example of 'English verdure, English culture' (360).

The long-term prospects for the more vital relationship that is established between Emma and her society at the Crown ball and during the excursion to Donwell are extremely promising. However, it does not bring her to any immediate sense of the restraints that must be placed on her fanciful treatment of outsiders, and discordant notes are introduced into each of these otherwise successful formal social occasions that suggest that such knowledge will be achieved, not as the end product of a gradual reintegration into her community, but through a sudden and very rude awakening. As a result of the kindness done to her by Mr Knightley at the Crown ball, Harriet Smith falls in love with him, and Emma's imagination is greatly stirred by hints that someone 'so superior to Mr Elton' (341) is now the object of her affections. Emma makes a great show of not interfering, and refuses to question Harriet as to the man's identity. However, this is only because she is sure that she already knows it. Frank Churchill has recently rescued Harriet in gallant and dramatic style from the gypsies, and given the romantic light in which she views her friend's affairs, it seems inevitable to Emma that she should have fallen in love with him. Conscious though she is of the value of Mr Knightley's intervention on Harriet's behalf at the ball, Emma does not consider for a moment that when her friend speaks of the 'inexpressible obligation' (342) she has incurred, she might be referring to an action that is so firmly based in the manners and morals of Highbury. Having forced Harriet once again into a romantic mould, Emma loses all sight of social reality and all sense of responsibility. Frank Churchill's rank and wealth make him an even less likely match than Mr Elton, yet Emma encourages Harriet to hope for a return of her affections. As a result of giving in to the demands of her imagination in this way, Emma sets in motion a chain of events, the culmination of which is to be a very sharp lesson in the consequences of failing to acknowledge consistently her obligations to others. Instead of a union between two people who exist only to amuse her, what eventually faces Emma is the possibility that she has helped create a match between Harriet and Mr Knightley which will not only destroy her own chances of happiness and fulfilment, but will undercut the prestige and authority of one of Highbury's leading citizens and thus damage the community.

This discordant note is reiterated, although very quietly, during the Donwell visit, and is mingled with the other louder ones sounded by Frank Churchill and Jane Fairfax. Because Emma has encouraged her to think that a match with Mr Knightley is not an impossibility, Harriet completely misinterprets his motives for singling her out for special attention during the walk through the grounds of the Abbey. Mr Knightley's intention is the very worthy one of reawakening Harriet's feelings for Robert Martin, but in fact he succeeds only in giving her the very improper impression that she is the object of his own affection. Since Emma has no way of knowing as yet that, like Frankenstein, she has lost control of her creation, and that Harriet is now spawning her own monstrous fantasies, she has little chance of recognising the dangers involved in the *tête-à-tête* that takes place at the end of the lime walk. This is not to say, however, that she could not still acquire the knowledge necessary to stop the process which is to end in a series of mortifying revelations, for there are other false notes sounded amidst the tranquil harmonies of Donwell that could be heard and interpreted by anyone willing to listen. Neither Jane Fairfax nor Frank Churchill acquiesces to the atmosphere of quietness and goodwill that Mr Knightley has tried to make the keynote of the day spent at his house. Jane leaves early and in a state of 'great agitation' (362); Frank Churchill arrives late and proves to be bad-tempered and restless. Both are distressed because of difficulties in their relationship, a situation which has been exacerbated by Emma's flirtation with Frank Churchill. Thus, a very clear hint is given that, by behaving irresponsibly in some areas, such as in her treatment of outsiders like Frank Churchill and Jane Fairfax, Emma will inevitably do harm in others even if, as is the case at Donwell, this runs directly counter to her conscious aims. The hint, however, is ignored, and it now becomes inevitable that Emma will achieve self-knowledge as the result of a painful exposure of the limitations of her inconsistent approach to experience.

A large part of this process of mortification must, of course, involve an unveiling of the misunderstanding, suffering and potential damage to Highbury that has been caused by Emma's manipulation of Harriet, Frank Churchill and Jane Fairfax. However, the essential flaw in Emma's view of the world is first exposed in another way, as an examination of the visit to Box Hill reveals. Box Hill, the only location in the novel that falls beyond the boundaries of Highbury, provides the ideal setting for Emma to indulge herself in an act so irresponsible and cruel that even she can grasp its significance. Unlike the Crown ball and the Donwell visit, in which the pursuit of novelty and entertainment operates within a context of propriety defined by the Highbury code of behaviour, the Box Hill excursion is intended to do nothing more than satisfy an idle desire for amusement on the part of Mrs Elton and Mr Weston. Because of this lack of responsible leadership, the excursion not only provides scope for disruptive behaviour, but also fails to achieve its immediate goal. Far from being a source of pleasure, the day is characterised by 'a languor, a want of spirits, a want of union' (367). Consequently, Emma quickly becomes bored, and lacking the restraints imposed on her during occasions conducted according to Highbury standards, she inevitably turns to her fantasy world for stimulation. Her attention is first directed at Frank Churchill, and she tries to titillate her jaded spirits by flirting with him. Frank, however, is not as responsive as usual and, desperate for amusement, Emma yields to her often felt but always resisted temptation to relegate Miss Bates to the status of outsider. What actually happens seems innocuous enough; Miss Bates makes a self-deprecating comment and Emma responds with a mildly insulting joke:

> 'I shall be sure to say three dull things as soon as ever I open my mouth . . .'
> Emma could not resist.
> 'Ah! ma'am, but there may be a difficulty. Pardon me—but you will be limited as to number—only three at once.'   (370)

Mr Knightley, however, explains the full implications of Emma's words:

> Were she a woman of fortune . . . I would not quarrel with you for any liberties of manner. Were she your equal in situation— but, Emma, consider how far this is from being the case. She is poor; she has sunk from the comforts she was born to; and, if she live to an old age, must probably sink more. Her situation should secure your compassion.   (375)

Emma's assumption that she has a right to entertain herself at Miss Bates' expense is, then, more than just an offence against a member of Highbury society, although even at this level it is inexcusable. Miss Bates has her origins within the upper reaches of the Highbury system of ranks, and the village's three leading families have committed themselves to ensuring that, in spite of her poverty and foolishness, she does not entirely lose her inherited position. By treating her as she does Emma directly contravenes this commitment.

Such an obvious abuse of what she has always acknowledged as being part of her duty brings Emma to the sudden realisation that those fanciful activities she has tried to reserve for what she considers peripheral areas of her life will inevitably have an effect on matters of the most intimate concern to her. Therefore, there is no room for even occasional deviations from Highbury norms. The lesson is repeated twice soon afterwards, first when the revelation of Frank Churchill's secret engagement to Jane Fairfax makes it clear what harm she has almost done to Miss Bates' niece, and, second, when she becomes convinced that she has created a match between Harriet and Mr Knightley. These mortifying discoveries help Emma grasp the full implications of her 'blindness of . . . head and heart' (411–12), and to understand how 'universally mistaken' she has been in her unpardonably arrogant schemes 'to arrange everybody's destiny' (413). However, the episode at Box Hill has been quite enough to bring Emma to the essential realisation that, if she is to remain within the moral limits of Highbury at all times, she must redefine her relationship to the community. The legitimate need for stimulation previously met by illegitimate means must be satisfied through a more whole-hearted commitment to the familiar, through a reaching beyond the tiny circle to which she has limited herself, and through a willingness to accept necessary change.

Thus, almost immediately after her return from Box Hill, Emma begins to display different attitudes. In the past 'a whole evening of back-gammon' (377) with Mr Woodhouse would have been merely tolerated as a necessary duty. Now, because of her recent experience, she has acquired a fresh sense of the value of situations that have nothing more to offer than good feeling, and she finds it a

> real pleasure, for there she was giving up the sweetest hours of the twenty-four to his [Mr Woodhouse's] comfort; and feeling that, unmerited as might be the degree of his fond affection and confiding esteem, she could not, in her general conduct, be open to any severe reproach. As a daughter, she hoped she was not without a heart.   (377)

A new spirit is also evident in Emma's decision to visit Miss Bates and in her attempts to be of use to Jane Fairfax during her illness. Instead of regarding them as people she would rather exclude from her area of concern, Emma is now eager to establish 'a regular, equal, kindly intercourse' (377) with Miss Bates, and has become 'sincerely interested' (379) in Jane Fairfax. Time spent in the Bates' house is thus no longer considered a tiresome obligation that must be lightened by excursions into fantasy. And, indeed, on this occasion far from making it easier to stay, thoughts of Jane's piano persuade her that it is time to leave:

> Now Emma was obliged to think of the piano-forté; and the remembrance of all her former fanciful and unfair conjectures was so little pleasing, that she soon allowed herself to believe her visit had been long enough; and, with a repetition of every thing

that she could venture to say of the good wishes which she really
felt, took leave.   (384)

Most indicative of Emma's new maturity, however, is the realisation that comes to her suddenly, although doubtless it owes a
great deal to her experiences at the Crown and Donwell, that she
can achieve complete fulfilment only if she is willing to accept
change and marry Mr Knightley:

> A mind like her's, once opening to suspicion, made rapid
> progress. She touched—she admitted—she acknowledged the
> whole truth . . . It darted through her, with the speed of an
> arrow, that Mr Knightley must marry no one but
> herself.   (407–8)

Now that her heroine has finally achieved self-knowledge and an
understanding of her proper social role, Jane Austen can bring her
action to its conclusion with Mr Knightley's marriage proposal.
Like Emma, he too has been shaken out of a contented lethargy by
the events of the past few months. Emma's flirtation with Frank
Churchill, and his own involvement in the Crown ball and the
Donwell visit, have served to make Mr Knightley reconsider his
situation in life, and to recognise that in order to complete himself he
must marry. The lesson that both Emma and Mr Knightley have
learned is summed up by what she experiences immediately after
accepting his proposal. The tea ceremony in which Emma takes
part is a familiar one but, by having involved herself in the kind of
responsible change that is possible without breaking prescribed
limits, she is able to apprehend it as something new:

> They sat down to tea—the same party round the same table—
> how often it had been collected!—and how often had her eyes
> fallen on the same shrubs in the lawn, and observed the same
> beautiful effect of the western sun!—But never in such a state of
> spirits, never in anything like it.   (434)

Highbury, then, seems sure to flourish under the leadership of two
people who understand the ways in which 'to go over the same
ground again' (435) can be made into an endlessly satisfying
experience, and the marriage of Emma and Mr Knightley, which is

the novel's last formal social occasion, becomes a symbol of the complete revitalisation of the once moribund village.

Emma's experience is a complicated one and the plot which embodies it is built upon a tangle of mysteries and confusions. However, Jane Austen organises her formal social occasions in such a way as to ensure that all aspects of it are brought into sharp focus, and the reader is left with a well-defined and subtle sense of the relationship between heroine and society, and of the changes which result on both sides from the interaction between them. Indeed, so successful is she in creating order out of the possible chaos of what is certainly her most intricate, if not her most complex, novel that *Emma* must be considered Jane Austen's greatest formal achievement.

6 Persuasion

By the time she wrote *Persuasion*, Jane Austen seems to have lost faith in the gentry. Sir Walter Elliot, the main representative of the class, is a man whose life has been reduced to 'a . . . vacuous ceremony'[1] by his conviction that rank and personal appearance are the only things that matter. He fails to acknowledge any obligations to his estate, and abandons it in favour of the idle pleasures of Bath rather than face up to the problem of paying off his debts. Since the heir to Kellynch is the more intelligent, but equally corrupt, William Walter Elliot, there seems little chance that the landed estate will ever again play the kind of role that it did in *Pride and Prejudice*, *Mansfield Park* and *Emma*. Given the serious questions that Jane Austen has asked about the old order in the two novels immediately preceding *Persuasion*, it is not entirely unexpected that she should finally find it beyond redemption. However, her analysis of the consequences of this decline is rather surprising.

The earlier novels have led us to expect that, should the old order fail, the power vacuum thus created would probably be filled by an essentially vulgar, self-seeking and materialistic bourgeoisie. Certainly, it is representatives of this group, in the shape of Isabella Thorpe, the Steele sisters, the Crawfords, and Mrs Elton who have always lurked around the fringes of, and sometimes offered threats to, the stability of Jane Austen's world. This does not turn out to be the case in *Persuasion*, however, for while Kellynch will become the property of a man concerned only with the self and money, there is no suggestion that William Walter Elliot represents the wave of the future. Rather, the future seems to lie in the hands of the navy, perhaps in a loose alliance with people like the Musgroves. Historically, such a forecast makes little sense. The British navy was not a separate interest group, which sought power for itself, but was simply an arm of the administration; the Musgroves are part of the old landed gentry. As such, they can only suggest that Jane Austen believed, quite wrongly as it turned out, in the possibility of a revitalisation of the old order from within. However, a closer look at the particular qualities with which Jane Austen endows the navy and the Musgroves makes it clear that she is using them in a rather special way which separates them from their expected class affiliations. The egalitarianism and strong family-feelings of the Musgroves, and the ability of the naval characters to reconcile the high value they place on work, profession and money with concern for the national interest, mark them not as bearers of traditional values but as an idealised bourgeoisie. To cast characters whom we would more obviously identify with the gentry in this role indicates a certain amount of equivocation on Jane Austen's part. She has recognised that things are changing, but is not yet ready to accept that power must pass into the hands of a middle class that she has previously characterised as being hostile to all the most basic human values.[2] One way around this unwillingness to admit that all is lost would be to accept the middle class at its own valuation. However, it is clearly more than Jane Austen can stomach to turn a Lucy Steele or a Mrs Elton into someone capable of reconciling individualism and the cash ethic with humanitarianism and a social conscience. What she does instead is to cobble together a somewhat fantasised version of the future in which the best aspects of the entrepreneurial ideal are embodied within groups of people for whom she has considerable sympathy.[3]

Even though Jane Austen has the courage to acknowledge that something has gone irretrievably wrong with her society, there is, then, a very strong escapist element in *Persuasion*. Only by recognising this can we understand why, in the middle of the novel, there is a sudden and remarkable transformation in the author's attitude to the breakdown in the structure of manners which is for her the main symptom of the passing of the old order. Throughout the first half of *Persuasion* Jane Austen is, as we might expect, extremely critical of a world in which manners no longer serve as a medium for moral communication. Someone like Anne Elliot, who is perhaps the finest of all Jane Austen's heroines, would have been greatly valued at Pemberley or in Highbury. However, because external display has become an end in itself at Kellynch, and because the people at Uppercross and Lyme lack a mature understanding of the importance of polite behaviour, she has great difficulty in establishing a place for herself in any of these communities. Anne's excellent manners in no way facilitate her lonely search for love and acceptance, and she has to wait for situations to occur which will give her the opportunity to prove herself by more active means. As it turns out, the child Charles's broken collar bone and Louisa Musgrove's fall from the Cobb do allow Anne to demonstrate her virtue, so that she finally wins the respect of the Musgroves and the Harvilles, and, most important, recaptures the love of Captain Wentworth. However, there is no sense of inevitability about this, as there is in the way that the earlier heroines are able to enter into harmonious relationships with their societies once they have corrected personal faults. On the contrary, since a woman's life is spent 'at home, quiet, confined' (232), for such chances to arise would appear to be the exception rather than the rule. Precisely how fortunate Anne has been can perhaps be gauged most accurately by considering the experience of the naval characters.[4] In contrast to women, sailors are 'forced on exertion' (232). Nevertheless, for every Captain Wentworth who has 'the good luck . . . to fall in with the very French frigate [he] wanted' (66) there are many others like the disabled Harville, Benwick, who was 'a year or two waiting for fortune and promotion' (96), and Sir Archibald Drew's grandson, for whom 'the peace has come too soon' (170), whose worth goes unrecognised.

Once the action shifts to Bath, however, Jane Austen ceases almost completely to express reservations about the prospect of living in a world dominated by people who lack any sophisticated knowledge of the language of manners. Suddenly, openness and goodwill become sufficient in themselves, and formality is shown to be not merely unnecessary but even synonymous with hypocrisy and alienation. In support of this conclusion, Jane Austen places great stress on the deficiencies of William Walter Elliot, whose excellent manners serve only to cover up his real depravity, and goes to some lengths to show how the demands of formality help to keep Anne and Wentworth apart. Nevertheless, her final position is unconvincing. The Musgroves and the naval characters are good people and, given our knowledge of her experience at Kellynch, we can sympathise with Anne Elliot's tendency to make light of their faults. All the same, these faults do exist, and the society into which Anne is entering remains too chaotic and disorganised to be considered an adequate substitute for such beautifully ordered worlds as Pemberley and Highbury. Thus, for the reader to agree with Anne that her new world is completely satisfactory would involve not only passing over much of what this novel has established, but also denying the value of the social structures which have been affirmed so definitely in the earlier novels.

A consideration of the thematic and structural role played by the formal social occasion in *Persuasion* helps us to grasp the extent to which the novel's conclusion reverses the direction of the preceding action. *Persuasion* is organised according to very simple but nonetheless effective principles. Three visits—to Uppercross, Lyme and Bath—are used to provide access to the novel's very distinct 'little social commonwealth [s]' (43). Thus, after beginning with a presentation of the decadent gentry at Kellynch, Jane Austen moves on to the alternative, but by no means perfect, worlds of Uppercross and Lyme. The novel is brought to its conclusion when the separate social groups converge on Bath, and the Elliots, whose life of sterile formality is played out in the public places of the city, are contrasted with the convivial, confused party which gathers in the privacy of the Musgroves' lodgings at the White Hart, and which includes the Crofts, the Harvilles and Captain Wentworth. This comparison, however, as I have already suggested, does not entirely confirm what has gone before. The Elliots, it now appears, are at fault, not just because they have lost sight of the point of formality, but because they are concerned with it at all; and the good-heartedness of the White Hart group is now presented as a more than adequate substitute for its lack of propriety. Thus, what began as a very qualified statement of preference for the less imperfect of two alternatives ends up as a buoyant assertion of the absolute superiority of the forces that are assuming control of English society.

The account of Sir Walter Elliot's way of life with which *Persuasion* opens demonstrates very forcibly the decadent condition into which Jane Austen believes the gentry has sunk. Sir Walter is very concerned with externals such as manners, social position, and personal appearance, but does not realise that they have value only so long as they reflect the moral concerns of the inner man. This causes him to misjudge completely the relative worth of his three daughters. Because Elizabeth is beautiful and Mary respectably married, he prefers them both to Anne, whose 'bloom had vanished early' (6). Yet Anne possesses 'an elegance of mind and sweetness of character, which must have placed her high with any people of real understanding' (5), while her sisters are both vain and foolish. Similarly, Sir Walter prefers the fortune-hunting Mrs Clay to the respectable and genuinely devoted Lady Russell simply because the former is younger and more attractive, and displays a suitably sycophantic respect for the importance of his social position. His attitude to Kellynch Hall is no better. For Sir Walter, the possession of a great house provides him with a source of prestige rather than duty. Therefore, he gains far more pleasure from rereading the record of his family's past glories in the Baronetage than from attending to the present obligations he owes to his estate and tenants. Sir Walter is so unaware that the high reputation of the landed gentleman derives from the very real function he is expected to perform that, when he is troubled by debts, he prefers to lose control of Kellynch rather than sacrifice any of the external marks of his rank:

> What! Every comfort of life knocked off! Journeys, London, servants, horses, table,—contractions and restrictions every where. To live no longer with the decencies even of a private gentleman! No, he would sooner quit Kellynch-hall at once, than remain in it on such disgraceful terms. (13)

Anne Elliot alone makes any consistent effort to persuade Sir Walter to acknowledge his responsibilities. So far as she is concerned the good name of the family can be preserved only by putting 'honesty' before 'importance' (12), and this involves making retrenchments and at all costs retaining control of Kellynch. However, she is 'nobody' (5) to Sir Walter, and can do nothing to influence his conduct.[5] Only in rare instances, such as at the moment of leave-taking, when Sir Walter's benign neglect allows her to perform the duties of a landlord herself, are Anne's attempts to preserve the respectability of the Elliots in the least successful: 'And one thing I have had to do, Mary, of a more trying nature; going to almost every house in the parish, as a sort of take-leave' (39). Clearly, this world has no role to offer Anne, and it is not her task to 'inherit' Kellynch in the sense that Fanny Price inherits Mansfield Park. Therefore, she takes her first step towards personal happiness and fulfilment when she decides to remain in the country rather than accompany Sir Walter and Elizabeth to Bath.

In setting out in search of a new community, Anne has no illusions about recapturing the ideal once represented by Kellynch. Her aim, rather, is the modest one of finding people who retain a basic concern for the needs of others and to whom she can be 'of some use' (33). Her limited expectations are made evident by a conversation she has with Sir Walter about the navy. Even allowing that his view is prejudiced and exaggerated, it is nevertheless evident from Sir Walter's comments that sailors are by and large men who lack refinement and good breeding. Such qualities, however, are far more than Anne expects, and the fact that they have served their country and demonstrated a willingness to work is quite enough to win her unstinting admiration:

> The navy, I think, who have done so much for us, have at least an equal claim with any other set of men, for all the comforts and all the privileges which any home can give. Sailors work hard enough for their comforts, we must all allow.   (19)

Considering the environment from which she has just escaped, and given her minimal expectations, it is not surprising that Anne discovers much that is admirable in Uppercross, the first of the new worlds that she is to encounter, and she soon expresses an ambition 'to become a not unworthy member of [the community] she was now transplanted into' (43). Unlike the Elliots, the Musgroves are a close and affectionate family:

> Anne always contemplated them [Henrietta and Louisa] as some of the happiest creatures of her acquaintance . . . and envied them . . . that seemingly perfect good understanding and agreement together, that good-humoured mutual affection, of which she had known so little herself with either of her sisters.   (41)

Furthermore, they are refreshingly unconcerned about the finer points of rank and formality. Charles Hayter's low social position, for example, provides no obstacle to his match with Henrietta, and the Musgrove sisters are extremely scornful of Mary's determination to take precedence over their mother:

> I have no scruple of observing to *you* [Anne], how nonsensical some persons are about their place, because, all the world knows how easy and indifferent you are about it: but I wish any body could give Mary a hint that it would be a great deal better if she were not so very tenacious; especially, if she would not be always putting herself forward to take place of mamma.   (46)

At this point in the novel, however, Jane Austen is not as

accepting of the Musgroves as Anne. By casting off 'the old English style' (40) before it became decadent they have been saved from the fate of the Elliots. Nevertheless, there is some question whether 'the state of alteration' in which we find them can really be equated with 'improvement' (40). For all that the egalitarianism and informality which are integral to this new style are to be preferred to the snobbish elegance of Kellynch, Jane Austen is willing to say no more than 'perhaps' (40). Her reservations are obvious. The 'stock of accomplishments' which the Musgrove sisters have acquired in the course of creating their 'modern minds and manners' (40) has given them a certain air of elegance. However, this is no substitute for the truly 'elegant and cultivated mind' (41) that could have been produced by a more solid traditional education and, like their brother Charles, who seems to have been subjected to even less intellectual discipline, Louisa and Henrietta prove to be essentially superficial and ignorant. Their main concern in life is to be 'happy, and merry' (40) and they have little attention to spare for more serious matters. They are particularly ignorant of the language of manners and therefore find it very difficult to communicate with or to assess the worth of anyone not embraced within the circle of family affection. As a result, the kind of 'order and neatness' which characterised life in the old society is replaced by an 'air of confusion' (40). This is very evident in the relationship between the inhabitants of the Great House and Mary Musgrove, who is a member of the family only through marriage. Even though 'the two families were so continually meeting, so much in the habit of running in and out of each other's houses at all hours' (36), there is little real communication between them and their dealings with each other are unnecessarily chaotic and acrimonious (44–6).

However, as the newest arrival at Uppercross, it is Anne Elliot who suffers most from the Musgroves' deficiencies. Her excellent manners do not count for any more here than they did at Kellynch, and she finds that she 'must now submit to feel that another lesson, in the art of knowing our own nothingness beyond our own circle, was become necessary for her' (42). The only role offered to Anne is that of 'umpire' (77) in Mary's many squabbles with Charles, Louisa, Henrietta, and Mrs Musgrove, but this merely emphasises her real isolation. Were she considered a part of one of the factions into which their world is divided, none of the Musgroves would feel safe in directing complaints at her.[6] Neither is it a role that allows Anne to be of any real use: 'How was Anne to set all these matters to rights? She could do little more than listen patiently, soften every grievance, and excuse each to the other' (46).

In a more mature society Anne would be able to prove her worth within the context of the formal social occasion. However, she is unable to play any meaningful part in social evenings at Uppercross because they are family affairs rather than mediums for polite intercourse. For example, even though she is an excellent pianist, Anne's playing is 'little thought of' by the uncomprehending and uninterested audience she encounters in the Musgroves' drawing room: 'She knew that when she played she was giving pleasure only to herself' (47). This is because, as Anne generously acknowledges, the Musgroves are typically much less concerned with the quality of the performance, which requires an objective judgement, than with their relationship to the performer: 'Mr and Mrs Musgrove's fond partiality for their own daughters' performance, and total indifference to any other person's, gave her much more pleasure for their sakes, than mortification for her own' (47).

The walk to Winthrop, the intention of which is to re-unite Henrietta and Charles Hayter, is also very much a family function, and again fails to provide Anne with any opportunities to demonstrate her abilities. For her, social intercourse amounts to nothing more satisfying than trying 'not to be in the way of anybody' and she experiences real enjoyment only when she directs her attention away from the group and towards nature: 'Her *pleasure* in the walk must arise from the exercise and the day, from the view of the last smiles of the year upon the tawny leaves and withered hedges' (84). Anne's reticence on this occasion, however, is very different from that which leads to Fanny Price's effective exclusion from the party visiting Sotherton. Whereas Fanny is too timid to claim a position that is rightfully hers. Anne is acutely and maturely aware that, as yet, this society has no position to offer her. In the first instance, the heroine is immature; in the second the social group.

Since her new world lacks any subtle understanding of the moral significance of the individual's polite performance, Anne must win the Musgrove's regard by actively demonstrating her usefulness and concern for others. To do this is not at all easy for a woman, however, especially one who has no clear function within the community, because her opportunities for exertion are inevitably limited. In all her visits to the Great House, for example, only on those few occasions when the evening ends in an 'unpremeditated little ball' is Anne able to do anything that is valued by her group:

'Anne, very much preferring the office of musician to a more active post, played country dances to them by the hour together; a kindness which always recommended her musical powers to the notice of Mr and Mrs Musgrove more than any thing else' (47). The normal routine of Uppercross life in fact throws up so few opportunities for Anne to prove her worth that it requires a freakish accident in which young Charles breaks his collarbone before she can reveal anything like the full extent of her considerable powers. Then, she takes complete charge of the situation and performs all the tasks necessary to alleviate the child's pain and restore order to a household thrown into confusion by Mary's collapse and the panic of the servants:

> It was an afternoon of distress, and Anne had every thing to do at once—the apothecary to send for—the father to have pursued and informed—the mother to support and keep from hysterics—the servants to control—the youngest child to banish, and the poor suffering one to attend and soothe.   (53)

The deficiencies of Uppercross ritual action are further exposed by Anne's first encounter with her former lover, Wentworth, at one of the Musgroves' evening parties. Had Anne been given a proper role to play by her group, she would inevitably have been forced into many situations in the course of this formal social occasion that would have facilitated a renewal of understanding and mutual affection between two people who are still essentially in love. As it is, however, the Musgroves place such a low value on Anne that she finds it easy to remain on the edge of the circle of involvement and thus avoid painful meetings with Wentworth: 'They had no conversation together, no intercourse but what the commonest civility required' (63). No one finds its inappropriate, for example, that Anne should exclude herself from the party gathered around Wentworth to hear of his adventures at sea. As a result, he is denied a fine opportunity to see that she is still deeply concerned for him: 'Anne's shudderings were to herself, alone' (66). Similarly, even though seated on the same settee as Wentworth and Mrs Musgrove, Anne is not asked to join in the conversation, and her feelings again remain private:

> they were divided only by Mrs Musgrove. It was no insignificant barrier indeed. Mrs Musgrove was of a comfortable substantial

size; and . . . the agitations of Anne's slender form, and pensive face, may be considered as very completely screened.   (68)

It is equally easy for Anne to avoid dancing with Wentworth because, by offering to play the piano, she is simply relegating herself to the peripheral position which the Musgroves have always felt to be appropriate for her. Once more, withdrawal from the group prevents the possibility of communication:

> On [dancing] being proposed, Anne offered her services, as usual, and though her eyes would sometimes fill with tears as she sat at the instrument, she was extremely glad to be employed, and desired nothing in return but to be unobserved.   (71)

The effect of these manoeuvres, which would not have been possible in a more sophisticated society, is to confirm Wentworth in his belief that he and Anne are now 'strangers' (64), and when they finally come face to face he treats her with cold formality:

> Unintentionally she returned to that part of the room; he saw her, and, instantly rising, said, with studied politeness,
>   'I beg your pardon, madam, this is your seat' and though she immediately drew back with a decided negative, he was not to be induced to sit down again.   (72)

As a consequence of this lack of ritual communication, there is every possibility that Anne and Wentworth's 'estrangement' will be 'perpetual' (64). This possibility is avoided only because, as was the case in Anne's relationship with the Musgroves, situations happen to occur that allow for a more direct communication than is possible within the formal context. Again, and perhaps to emphasise the parallel, Jane Austen ventures into the unpredictable world of the child. Wentworth's visit to Uppercross Cottage seems unlikely at first to do anything to alter the pattern set by his previous encounter with Anne because each hides behind a barrier of polite trivialities. However, when the child Walter climbs on Anne's back, Wentworth steps forward and removes him, thus demonstrating in a quite practical way that, despite his feelings of resentment, he is still sensitive to her needs. The gesture is so spontaneous that Wentworth probably does not grasp its significance. Nevertheless, Anne is acutely conscious of what his action means:

Her sensations on the discovery made her perfectly speechless. She could not even thank him. She could only hang over little Charles, with most disordered feelings. His kindness in stepping forward to her relief . . . produced such a confusion of varying, but very painful agitation.   (80)

A second, and similar, incident occurs at the end of the walk to Winthrop. This group function, like the earlier evening party, has done nothing to bring Anne closer to Wentworth. On the contrary, since it includes the mortifying episode in which Anne overhears Wentworth expressing genuine affection for Louisa Musgrove, it has tended to force them further apart. However, an unexpected meeting with the Crofts suddenly creates a situation that is more than merely ritual. The rest of the party assumes that Admiral Croft's offer to drive home any lady that might be tired has been 'generally declined' (90) even though only Louisa, Henrietta and Mary have made their wishes known. But before the Crofts can leave, Wentworth asks Mrs Croft to extend the invitation specifically to Anne. By so doing he demonstrates once more that he is aware of Anne's needs—for she is indeed 'tired' (90)—and is willing to meet these needs. Again, Anne is alert to the significance of Wentworth's gesture: 'still he could not see her suffer, without the desire of giving her relief. It was a remainder of former sentiment; it was an impulse of pure, though unacknowledged friendship; it was a proof of his own warm and amiable heart' (91).

The trip to Lyme takes Anne into a social milieu which is superior to that of Uppercross. Hints of this have already been given by a conversation between the Crofts and Wentworth at the Musgroves' evening party. Mrs Croft's account of her preference for remaining with her husband even during his voyages suggests that naval people are as capable of warm family feelings as the Musgroves:

While we were together, you know, there was nothing to be feared . . . The only time that I ever really suffered in body or mind, the only time that I ever fancied myself unwell, or had any ideas of danger, was the winter that I passed by myself at Deal.   (70–1)

But it also appears that sailors have developed a professional ethic that enables them to extend their area of concern somewhat beyond that of the Musgroves. Thus, Wentworth asserts that 'I would assist any brother officer's wife that I could, and I would bring any thing of Harville's from the world's end, if he wanted it' (69). This excellent impression is completely confirmed by the small community of sailors that has been formed in Lyme. Although they are living in temporary accommodation and have little spare cash, the Harvilles have nevertheless transformed their lodgings into a warm, family dwelling.[7] Theirs is not a closed world, however. By adding 'some few articles of a rare species of wood, excellently worked up, and . . . something curious and valuable from all the distant countries [he] had visited,' to the 'common necessaries provided by the owner', Captain Harville has produced a 'picture of repose and domestic happiness' that is 'connected . . . with his profession, the fruit of its labours, the effect of its influence on his habits' (98). His rooms, then, are as much an emblem of naval values as familial, and can offer space to a distressed comrade like Benwick and a hospitable welcome to Captain Wentworth. Such companionableness is possible because Harville, Benwick and Wentworth are all committed to the same professional standards, and each admires the way the others have performed their national duty. When Wentworth describes Benwick as 'an excellent young man and an officer' (96), he means in effect that he is an excellent young man because he is an excellent officer.

Anne Elliot finds herself in complete sympathy with these people who are characterised by 'friendliness . . . brotherliness . . . openness . . . uprightness' and is not far from sharing Louisa Musgrove's view that sailors possess 'more worth and warmth than any other set of men in England' (99). Certainly she would consider herself well placed were she included in their community:

> There was so much attachment to Captain Wentworth in all this, and such a bewitching charm in a degree of hospitality so uncommon, so unlike the usual style of give-and-take invitations, and dinners of formality and display, that Anne felt her spirits not likely to be benefited by an increasing acquaintance among his brother-officers. 'These would have been all my friends,' was her thought; and she had to struggle against a great tendency to lowness.   (98)

However, admirable as the naval characters may be, Jane Austen makes it clear that, like the Musgroves, they fall short of the ideal

achieved in her earlier novels. Because of the demands of active
service, sailors are unable to establish permanent homes or to
conduct well-regulated lives, and so are deprived of opportunities to
gain an understanding of the finer points of social intercourse. A full
knowledge of manners, for example, depends on having paid keen
attention to the way in which people respond to the reiterated and
unchanging patterns of the formal social occasion. It is thus hardly
likely to be achieved by a man like Wentworth whose main energies
are directed not into orderly rituals but towards enterprises so
unpredictable that they could equally well make his fortune or leave
him dead: 'I knew that we should either go to the bottom together,
or that she [the *Asp*] would be the making of me' (65–6). As a result
sailors are not skilled or even very interested in communicating with
those who fall outside their immediate circle. Though he is master of
Kellynch, Admiral Croft does not entertain formally, and the
Harvilles express no qualms at remaining in Lyme after the season
has ended: 'They were come too late in the year for any amusement
or variety which Lyme, as a public place, might offer; the rooms
were shut up' (95). They prefer, instead, to meet informally with
other members of the naval profession. Harville, therefore, is eager
that Wentworth should dine with him, and during his visit to Bath,
Croft is usually to be seen in the street 'forming into a little knot of
the navy' (168) rather than in the public rooms.

These limitations make themselves felt in a number of small ways.
Admiral Croft, for example, has such difficulty seeing beyond his
family and the navy that he tends to forget any female name other
than his wife's: 'I wish young ladies had not such a number of fine
christian names. I should never be out, if they were all Sophys, or
something of that sort' (171). Croft also runs into problems in trying
to reconcile his good opinion of Benwick with young man's limited
success in the navy:

> Oh! yes, yes, there is not a word to be said against James Benwick.
> He is only a commander, it is true, made last summer, and these
> are bad times for getting on, but he has not another fault that I
> know of. An excellent, good-hearted fellow, I assure
> you.   (171)

However, as was the case with the Musgroves, the inadequacies of
the naval group are made most apparent by their dealings with
Anne Elliot. As a member of Wentworth's party, she is warmly

greeted by the Harvilles, but is granted little importance in her own right. Therefore, during a social evening at the Harvilles' lodgings, 'Captains Wentworth and Harville led the talk at one side of the room' while Anne is 'placed rather apart' (100) with the low-spirited Benwick.

Clearly, then, good manners will not be enough to gain Anne entry into either the Musgrove or the naval groups, and she is very fortunate that an incident sufficiently testing to make her virtue evident to all should occur during the second day of the visit to Lyme. Lack of proper restraint and self-discipline on the part of Louisa and her companions, Musgroves and sailors, are responsible both for her fall from the Cobb and for their failure to react appropriately to it. Only Anne has the 'strength and zeal, and thought' (111) that the situation requires, and while the rest of the party panics, she responds immediately to Wentworth's anguished cry for help:

'Is there no one to help me?' were the first words which burst from Captain Wentworth, in a tone of despair, and as if all his own strength were gone.

'Go to him, go to him,' cried Anne, 'for heaven's sake go to him. I can support her myself.'   (110)

Even after all attempts to arouse Louisa have failed, Anne continues to act with firmness and decision:

Louisa was raised up and supported more firmly between them, and every thing was done that Anne prompted, but in vain; while Captain Wentworth, staggering against the wall for his support, exclaimed in the bitterest agony,

'Oh God! her father and mother!'

'A surgeon!' said Anne.

He caught the word; it seemed to rouse him at once, and saying only 'True, true, a surgeon this instant,' was darting away, when Anne eagerly suggested,

'Captain Benwick, would not it be better for Captain Benwick? He knows where a surgeon is to be found.'   (110)

By taking control of the situation so decisively Anne at last demonstrates not just that she is worthy of a place in the group, but that, like an adult amongst good-natured but rather helpless

children, she is indispensible to it. Thus, she moves in one step from
the edge of the community to its centre. From this point on, far from
ignoring Anne, her companions, including Charles Musgrove and
Captain Wentworth, the two males leading the party, treat her with
something approaching deference:

> '"Anne, Anne," cried Charles, "what is to be done next? What,
> in heaven's name, is to be done next?"
> Captain Wentworth's eyes were also turned towards
> her.' (111)

Similarly, Wentworth asks Anne's approval before proceeding with
his plan for breaking the news of Louisa's accident to her parents:
'"Do you think this is a good plan?"
She did: he was satisfied, and said no more' (117). The elder
Musgroves become so dependent on Anne that when she decides to
return to Lyme, they ask rather pathetically, 'What should they do
without her?' (122). In its outcome, then, the Cobb incident is very
satisfying for Anne, but it leaves no doubts that the world into which
she has just gained entry is a very imperfect one. Louisa's fall would
never have happened in a better-ordered society, and it certainly
would not have needed such a freakish accident before the worth of
someone of such obviously superior qualities as Anne could be
recognised.

It now requires only Wentworth's marriage proposal to complete
Anne's journey in search of a new home. And were this proposal to
have been made immediately after the events at Lyme, and the
novel brought to its conclusion without the introduction of the Bath
episode, it would not have been difficult to understand how Jane
Austen felt about the process of social change. Up to this point in
Persuasion, she has been concerned to show that the consequences of
the breakdown of the old order are by no means totally disastrous,
because power is passing into the hands of a group of people
characterised by warm feelings and a genuine concern for the needs
of others. Nevertheless, Jane Austen has also made it very clear that
before it reduced manners to a medium for worthless display, this
old order represented an ideal of civilised existence far beyond
anything the Musgroves or the sailors could hope to achieve. The
novel has therefore been infused with a deep sense of loss. However,
Persuasion does not end with the visit to Lyme, and the Bath episode

confuses the issue considerably because it completely lacks this elegiac note. Instead, it suggests that the openness and spontaneity that characterise Anne's new world are adequate to any situation, and questions whether, even at its best, a society based on ritual forms of communication has any value.

Much of the argument of the last section of *Persuasion* is contained within Jane Austen's presentation of that self-conscious manipulator of manners, William Walter Elliot, whose concept of duty is ' "To do the best for himself" ' (202). To all appearances, Mr Elliot is an excellent person, possessed of a combination of personal and social accomplishments that approach the ideal set by a Darcy or a Mr Knightley:

> Every thing united in him; good understanding, correct opinions, knowledge of the world, and a warm heart. He had strong feelings of family-attachment and family-honour, without pride or weakness; he lived with the liberality of a man of fortune, without display; he judged for himself in every thing essential, without defying public opinion in any point of worldly decorum.   (146)

As it turns out, though, the refined performance which creates this impression is nothing more than a mask which lifts off to expose Mr Elliot as a gross hypocrite and a selfish exploiter. With the addition of this portrait to the one of Sir Walter Elliot, Jane Austen's analysis of corrupt formality darkens considerably. Sir Walter's manners are extremely offensive because they serve only to aggrandise the self. However, they also do nothing to conceal the reality of the man or his intentions. Anne is pained, for example, by Sir Walter's toadying reception of the Dalrymples, but is not in any way misled by it. Mr Elliot, on the other hand, shows that manners need neither demonstrate a concern for others nor be a useful guide to the inner man. There are, of course, manipulators of polite forms in Jane Austen's earlier novels, but they do not carry quite the same weight as Mr Elliot. Whereas they clearly deviate from a norm of good manners embodied within another character or characters, he is the most refined person that Anne meets, and therefore comes dangerously close to representing the norm. Moreover, none of these other hypocrites can take in any but those willing to be deceived. Emma, for example, may not be able to see through Frank Churchill, but Mr Knightley can. Yet, even Anne Elliot, an extremely intelligent and rational person who is predisposed to think rather badly of Mr Elliot, is unable to penetrate his façade.

However, the shift in Jane Austen's attitude to manners is still more fundamental than this. Anne rejects Mr Elliot long before Mrs Smith reveals the full truth about him, on the grounds that his very concern with polite forms is enough to diminish him as a human being:

> Mr Elliot was rational, discreet, polished,—but he was not open. There was never any burst of feeling, any warmth of indignation or delight, at the evil or good of others. This, to Anne, was a decided imperfection. Her early impressions were incurable. She prized the frank, the open-hearted, the eager character beyond all others.   (161)

There is no indication that Jane Austen disagrees with her heroine's judgement, and yet implicit within it is a denial of much of what she has asserted in her earlier novels. One of her main concerns in *Sense and Sensibility*, for example, is to disabuse Marianne Dashwood of the very similar notion that, in order to stay within the bounds of decorum, the individual must suppress some of the more vigorous and spontaneous aspects of his personality.

In the first part of *Persuasion*, Jane Austen argues that when a society's system of manners breaks down people find it more difficult to communicate with each other. During the Bath section, however, she begins to suggest that were it not for the demands of formality, communication would be easy. Anne and Wentworth, for example, as a result of their experiences in Lyme, need only to spend some time together in order to achieve mutual understanding. But, hard as each tries, they are repeatedly foiled by quite proper requirements of good manners. Thus, when Anne spots Wentworth through the window of a shop, she goes out of her way to attract his attention: 'She now felt a great inclination to go to the outer door; she wanted to see if it rained. Why was she to suspect herself of another motive? Captain Wentworth must be out of sight' (175). And he too is ready to take advantage of this chance encounter: 'After a short interval, however, he came towards her and spoke again' (176). However, when Wentworth tries to prolong their conversation by offering to escort Anne home, she is obliged to subordinate the dictates of her feelings to those of correct form and refuse him because she has already accepted a similar invitation from Mr Elliot.

Wentworth and Anne's first formal encounter in Bath—at the benefit concert—proves to be equally frustrating. Their natural inclination is to gravitate towards each other, and they do in fact manage a brief snatch of conversation about Lyme and about Benwick's engagement to Louisa that provides Anne with some clear hints of Wentworth's feelings for her:

> Anne, who, in spite of the agitated voice in which the latter part had been uttered, and in spite of all the various noises of the room, the almost ceaseless slam of the door, and ceaseless buzz of persons walking through, had distinguished every word, was struck, gratified, confused, and beginning to breathe very quick, and feel an hundred things in a moment.   (183)

However, Anne is soon separated from Wentworth by her obligation to pay 'needful civilities' (184) to Lady Dalrymple and her party. During the concert itself Anne must sit with the Dalrymple group from which Wentworth is excluded, and is 'so surrounded and shut in' (188) by it that he cannot even draw near to her.

As was the case in the shop, Mr Elliot profits most from this artificial division between the lovers, and manages to occupy Anne's attention for most of the evening. Even when Anne does finally manoeuvre herself into Wentworth's company, the demands of politeness almost immediately force her to return her attention to Mr Elliot:

> They talked for a few minutes more; the improvement held; he even looked down towards the bench, as if he saw a place on it well worth occupying; when, at that moment, a touch on her shoulder obliged Anne to turn round.—It came from Mr Elliot. He begged her pardon, but she must be applied to, to explain Italian again. Miss Carteret was very anxious to have a general idea of what was next to be sung. Anne could not refuse; but never had she sacrificed to politeness with a more suffering spirit.   (190)

This incident makes Wentworth so jealous that he flees the proceedings, leaving Mr Elliot to enjoy Anne's company unchallenged. However, since she has little regard for the ritual, Anne does not pay any heed to the patterns of movement it creates; the formal social occasion has no significance beyond itself and so cannot be a microcosm of the individual's larger intentions. What Anne considers important is not that Mr Elliot has won the polite battle for her company, but that within the interstices of the evening there have been private conversations and spontaneous displays of feeling which have given clear indications that Wentworth is in love with her.

Jane Austen completes her rejection of formality when the action of the novel switches to the Musgroves' lodgings at the White Hart. Here, amidst an atmosphere of 'thorough confusion' (221) created by 'the unaffected, easy kindness of manner' (231) of 'such men as have hearts' (235) we are far from the world of 'elegant stupidity' (180). Sir Walter's patronising invitation to an evening party goes for little in this setting ' "Phoo! phoo!" replied Charles, "what's an evening party? Never worth remembering"' (223). And the appearance of Sir Walter himself in support of his invitation causes 'a general chill' to spread over the room: 'The comfort, freedom, the gaiety of the room was over, hushed into cold composure, determined silence, or insipid talk, to meet the heartless elegance of her father and sister' (226). In this context 'open-hearted communication' (230) and 'generous attachment' (185) are at last possible. The inability of the Musgroves and the sailors to read the language of manners no longer causes problems, and explicit statement becomes a satisfactory substitute for polite communication. Thus, for Anne to express an aversion to attending the private party at which Mr Elliot is to be one of the most important guests is enough to relieve Wentworth of his feelings of jealousy. Similarly, Anne's extended and extremely pointed defence of female fidelity is all that is needed to convince Wentworth that she has indeed remained faithful to him during eight apparently hopeless years.

Jane Austen, then, has turned her novel almost completely around. During the Bath section she has emphasised how easy ritual forms of social intercourse make it for the hypocrite to conceal his intentions, and has suggested that even when entered into responsibly they limit the individual and hinder communication. The breakdown of a society structured around a sophisticated system of manners therefore no longer seems so disastrous, especially as it is being replaced by one that cultivates openness and informality. For Anne to become part of the Musgrove-naval world now appears to be entirely desirable, and the scene surrounding Wentworth's marriage proposal is infused with a spirit of optimism:

> There could be only a most proper alacrity, a most obliging compliance for public view; and smiles reined in and spirits dancing in private rapture. In half a minute, Charles was at the bottom of Union-street again, and the other two proceeding together; and soon words enough had passed between them to decide their direction towards the comparatively quiet and retired gravel-walk, where the power of conversation would make the present hour a blessing indeed; and prepare for it all the immortality which the happiest recollections of their own future lives could bestow.   (240)

The ritual suggested here by the dance metaphor is entirely private, and it is played out against the shifting and anonymous background of the street. However, this has become enough for Jane Austen and she refuses to recognise that anything, other than the dangers of war, could possibly compromise the happiness of Anne's future as a member of 'that profession which is, if possible, more distinguished in its domestic virtues than in its national importance' (252).

Because of its author's equivocation, *Persuasion* is fractured into two rather contradictory halves. As an artistic unity it is thus inferior to such perfectly structured and coherent works as *Pride and Prejudice*, *Emma* and *Mansfield Park*. However, in none of these novels does Jane Austen have to deal with the painful realisation that the social order which it has been the business of her literary career to explore and vindicate is finally falling apart. Since her novels owe their form as well as their theme to the structure of her society, it is hardly surprising that its collapse should lead to an at least partial collapse of her art.

Notes

INTRODUCTION: THE NOVELS AND THEIR WORLD

1. *Some Words of Jane Austen* (Chicago: University of Chicago Press, 1973) p. xi. Tave's discussion of the word 'lively' can be found in his chapter on Fanny Price, pp. 158–204.

2. The terms aristocracy, gentry and middle class will recur throughout my discussion of Jane Austen's novels. I use them in accordance with the definitions established by G. E. Mingay, *English Landed Society in the Eighteenth Century* (London: Routledge and Kegan Paul, 1963) pp. 19–49, and Harold Perkin, *The Origins of Modern English Society, 1780–1880* (London: Routledge and Kegan Paul, 1969) pp. 17–62. Both Mingay and Perkin argue that the crucial division in eighteenth-century society was between those who lived almost entirely off their rents, that is, the landlords, and those who had to work for a living, whether on the land or in towns.

   The landlords can be divided into two main groups.

   (1) *The great landlords.* Since title followed property in the eighteenth century, these were almost entirely the peers, and form the group which I call the aristocracy. According to Mingay, the essential status symbols of the great landlords were 'the great house and the London season' (19). These could not be afforded on an income of less than £5000–£6000 a year in 1790. Only 400 families belonged to this group and their average income was £10,000 a year. (2) *The lesser landlords or gentry.* Mingay breaks this group down into three subdivisions. (a) *The wealthy gentry.* They had an income of £3000–£4000 a year, and there were perhaps 700 or 800 families in this income range, mainly those of baronets and knights and some of untitled gentlemen. (b) *The lesser gentry.* They had an income of £1000–£3000 a year, and included a few knights, but the vast majority were plain country squires, in all perhaps 3000 or even 4000 families. (c) *The modest gentry.* They had an income of £300–£1000, and there were perhaps 15,000 or more families in this category. Perkin's divisions are consistent with Mingay's, but he pitches the average income of the great landlords at £8000 a year in 1803, the wealthy gentry at £3000 and the lesser gentry at £1500. Perkin also points out that members of the higher professions, such as the clergyman, the physician and the barrister, were usually included amongst the gentry.

   The middle classes embraced a tremendous range of incomes and occupations but were 'distinguished at the top from the gentry and nobility not so much by lower incomes as by the necessity of earning their living, and at the bottom from the labouring poor not so much by higher incomes as by the property, however small, represented by stock in trade, livestock, tools, or the educational investment of skill and expertise' (Perkin, p. 23). At the top of this group were the great overseas merchants who vied in wealth with many peers, and at the bottom the small farmers and semi-independent craftsmen with an annual income of around £100.

Below the three ranks with which Jane Austen deals were the lower orders which consisted of those who lacked property or special skills. They ranged from artisans with an income of £55 a year to vagrants with £10.

According to Perkin, in 1803 the landlords made up 1.4 per cent of all families and received 15.7 per cent of the national income; the middle class were 31.6 per cent of families and received 59.4 per cent of the national income; and the lower orders comprised 67 per cent of families and had 24.9 per cent of the national income.

3. Perkin, p. 51.
4. 'Some Reflections on Social History in the Nineteenth Century', *Victorian Studies*, 4 (1960) 58.
5. Asa Briggs, *The Age of Improvement, 1783–1867* (London: Longman, 1959) p. 101.
6. *Reflections on the Revolution in France, Works*, Vol. v (London: Rivington, 1803–27) p. 100.
7. Perkin, p. 55.
8. *Reflections on the Revolution in France, Works*, v, p. 181.
9. Perkin, p. 50.
10. *First Letter on a Regicide Peace, Works*, VIII, p. 172.
11. Thomas Gisborne argues that an important part of the woman's social role is taken up with 'forming and improving the general manners, dispositions, and conduct of the other sex, by society and example'. See *An Inquiry into the Duties of the Female Sex* (London: Cadell and Davies, 1801) p. 12.

Mrs West argues in similar vein: 'To these domestic duties and obligations, may be added what belongs to us in the aggregate, as the refiners of manners, and the conservators of morals.' See, *Letters to a Young Lady* (London: Longman, 1806) Vol. 1 p. 56.
12. All references to Jane Austen's novels are included in the text and are taken from R. W. Chapman (ed.), *The Novels of Jane Austen*, 3rd ed. (Oxford: Oxford University Press, 1933); Vol. 1, *Sense and Sensibility*; Vol. 2, *Pride and Prejudice*; Vol. 3, *Mansfield Park*; Vol. 4, *Emma*; Vol. 5, *Northanger Abbey* and *Persuasion*. Vol. 6, *Minor Works* was published in 1954. The title of the novel is cited in the text only when the reference would otherwise be unclear.
13. *The Social Dances of the Nineteenth Century in England* (London: Herbert Jenkins, 1960) pp. 22–3.
14. Quoted from Rosamund Bayne-Powell, *Travellers in Eighteenth-Century England* (London: John Murray, 1951) pp. 136–7.
15. See, for example, Donald Greene, 'The Myth of Limitation', in Joel Weinsheimer (ed.), *Jane Austen Today* (Athens: University of Georgia Press, 1975) pp. 142–75.
16. It might be objected that Jane Austen did not so much choose her subject matter as simply use what she knew best. However in her case, to write about what she knew best involved a great deal of choice. In setting out on her literary career, Jane Austen's most obvious course of action would have been to have followed the example set by the Gothic novel, which was at the height of

its popularity in the 1790s. Had she done so, then she would have written about the unfamiliar rather than the familiar. The kind of critical thinking that went into Jane Austen's decision to locate her novels in rural England rather than 'Italy, Switzerland, and the South of France', is made very evident in *Northanger Abbey*: 'Charming as were all Mrs Radcliffe's works, and charming even as were the works of all her imitators, it was not in them perhaps that human nature, at least in the midland counties of England, was to be looked for' (200).

17. R. W. Chapman (ed.), *Jane Austen's Letters* (London: Oxford University Press, 1952) p. 401.

18. R. W. Chapman argues that Jane Austen's own position within the gentry explains her tendency to proclaim the moral superiority of this group. See, *Jane Austen: Facts and Problems* (Oxford: Clarendon Press, 1948) pp. 198–9.

19. See Perkin, pp. 218–339.

20. *The Rites of Passage*, trans. Monika B. Vizedom and Gabrielle L. Caffee (Chicago: University of Chicago Press, 1960) p. 3.

21. We cannot, of course, be entirely sure of the order in which Jane Austen's first three novels were composed. However, in following the sequence *Northanger Abbey, Sense and Sensibility, Pride and Prejudice* I am consistent with the most exhaustive study of the topic, that of B. C. Southam, *Jane Austen's Literary Manuscripts. A Study of the Novelist's Development through the Surviving Papers* (London: Oxford University Press, 1964) pp. 53–63. Southam points out that, although Jane Austen had written versions of *Sense and Sensibility* and *Pride and Prejudice* prior to beginning work on *Northanger Abbey* in 1798, nevertheless this is the first novel she finished. Thus, *Northanger Abbey* was largely completed in 1799, whereas the process by which *Elinor and Marianne* (1797) became what we now know as *Sense and Sensibility* was not ended until 1809–10, and that by which *First Impressions* (1796–7) became *Pride and Prejudice* was not completed until 1812. *Pride and Prejudice*, in particular, seems to have undergone extensive revisions in 1809–10, 1811 and 1812.

There seems no reason to doubt the evidence offered by Jane Austen's sister, Cassandra, that *Mansfield Park* was composed 1811–13, *Emma*, 1814–15 and *Persuasion*, 1815–16. Southam (136–48) convincingly dismisses the claims made by Q. D. Leavis, 'A Critical Theory of Jane Austen's Writings', *Scrutiny*, 10 (1941) 61–90, 114–42, (1942) 272–94; 12 (1944) 104–19, that *Mansfield Park* and *Emma* have their origins in the earlier uncompleted works *Lady Susan* (*ca.* 1793–4) and *The Watsons* (1804–5).

22. This is not to deny that my study is greatly indebted to previous critics of Jane Austen. Since I do not intend to engage in a lengthy debate with other critics this might be an appropriate point at which to acknowledge those scholars who are most pertinent to my particular approach.

My knowledge of Jane Austen's relationship to her age has been informed by Marilyn Butler, *Jane Austen and the War of Ideas* (Oxford: Clarendon Press, 1975); Alistair M. Duckworth, *The Improvement of the Estate: A Study of Jane Austen's Novels* (Baltimore: The Johns Hopkins Press, 1971); Joseph M. Duffy, Jr, 'Structure and Idea in Jane Austen's *Persuasion*', *Nineteenth Century Fiction*, 8 (1954) pp. 272–89; Avrom Fleishman, *A Reading of 'Mansfield Park': An Essay in Critical Synthesis* (Minneapolis: University of Minnesota Press, 1967); D. W. Harding, 'Regulated Hatred: An Aspect of the Work of Jane Austen',

Scrutiny, 8 (1940) 346–62; Richard Poirier, 'Mark Twain, Jane Austen, and the Imagination of Society', in R. A. Brower and R. Poirier (eds), *In Defense of Reading: A Reader's Approach to Literary Criticism* (New York: Dutton, 1962) pp. 282–309; E. Rubinstein, 'Jane Austen's Novels: The Metaphor of Rank', in Eric Rothstein and Richard N. Ringler (ed.), *Literary Monographs*, Vol. II (Madison: University of Wisconsin Press, 1969) pp. 101–93, 218–25; B. C. Southam, '*Sanditon*: The Seventh Novel', in Juliet McMaster (ed.), *Jane Austen's Achievement*, (London: Macmillan, 1976) pp. 1–26; Tony Tanner, 'Jane Austen and "The Quiet Thing"—A Study of *Mansfield Park*', in B. C. Southam (ed.) *Critical Essays on Jane Austen* (London: Routledge and Kegan Paul, 1968) pp. 136–61; Raymond Williams, *The English Novel: From Dickens to Lawrence* (London: Chatto and Windus, 1970) pp. 18–24; Raymond Williams, *The Country and the City* (London: Chatto and Windus, 1973).

On the topic of manners, the following are particularly important. Howard S. Babb, *Jane Austen's Novels: The Fabric of Dialogue* (Columbus: Ohio State University Press, 1962); Susan Morgan, 'Polite Lies: The Veiled Heroine of *Sense and Sensibility*', *Nineteenth-Century Fiction*, 31 (1976) 188–205; Jane Nardin, *Those Elegant Decorums: The Concept of Propriety in Jane Austen's Novels* (Albany: State University of New York Press, 1973); Martin Price, 'Manners, Morals, and Jane Austen', *Nineteenth-Century Fiction*, 30 (1975) 261–80; Lionel Trilling, 'Manners, Morals and the Novel', in *The Liberal Imagination* (London: Secker and Warburg, 1951) pp. 205–22.

A few critics have paid attention to social groups and rituals, including Langdon Elsbree, 'Jane Austen and the Dance of Fidelity and Complaisance', *Nineteenth-Century Fiction*, 15 (1960) 113–36; Barbara Hardy, *A Reading of Jane Austen* (London: Peter Owen, 1975) pp. 103–35; Francis R. Hart, 'The Spaces of Privacy: Jane Austen', *Nineteenth-Century Fiction*, 30 (1975) 305–33.

My knowledge of Jane Austen's society owes a lot to the books by Harold Perkin, G. E. Mingay and Asa Briggs already cited in the notes. Others who have contributed are Ford K. Brown, *Fathers of the Victorians: The Age of Wilberforce* (Cambridge: Cambridge University Press, 1961); William Cobbett, *Rural Rides* (1830; new edition Harmondsworth: Penguin, 1967); Élie Halévy, *England in 1815* (London: E. Benn, 1961); Charles Parkin, *The Moral Basis of Burke's Political Thought* (Cambridge: Cambridge University Press, 1956); E. P. Thompson, *The Making of the English Working Class* (London: Victor Gollancz, 1963); F. M. L. Thompson, *English Landed Society in the Nineteenth Century* (London: Routledge and Kegan Paul, 1963).

1 NORTHANGER ABBEY

1. Of the many studies of *Northanger Abbey* as a novel about fiction, perhaps the most comprehensive is Katrin Ristkok Burlin, ' "The Pen of the Contriver": The Four Fictions in *Northanger Abbey*', in John Halperin (ed.), *Jane Austen: Bicentenary Essays* (Cambridge: Cambridge University Press, 1975) pp. 89–111.

2. Those who have placed *Northanger Abbey* in the mainstream of Jane Austen's fiction include Butler, pp. 172–81; Duckworth, pp. 92–101; George Levine, 'Translating the Monstrous: *Northanger Abbey*', *Nineteenth-Century Fiction*, 30 (1975) 335–50; B. C. Southam, '*Sanditon*: The Seventh Novel', pp. 1–14.

3. Darrell Mansell, *The Novels of Jane Austen: An Interpretation* (London: Macmillan, 1973) p. 36, has also recognised that the Tilney-Thorpe opposition plays an important part in the structure of *Northanger Abbey*.
4. Of the many critics who have been misled into underrating Catherine Morland, the most extreme is Marvin Mudrick who dismisses her as a 'matter-of-fact ingénue'. See *Jane Austen: Irony as Defense and Discovery* (Princeton: Princeton University Press, 1952) p. 57. Tave, p. 42, and Joseph Wiesenfarth, *The Errand of Form: An Assay of Jane Austen's Art* (New York: Fordham University Press, 1967) p. 26, have recognised that Catherine is capable of learning. However, Tave tends to damn her with faint praise.
5. This similarity between General Tilney and the Thorpes has also been pointed out by Babb, pp. 94–5.

2 SENSE AND SENSIBILITY

1. For a discussion of Jane Austen's presentation of Elinor's inner life, see Butler, pp. 189–90.
2. Many critics have commented on the inadequate presentation of Edward Ferrars and Colonel Brandon. See, for example, Mudrick, pp. 86–90. Several critics, however, have realised that they are intended to play an important role in the novel. Duckworth, p. 111, comments that Brandon and Ferrars are characterised by 'commitment to their roles'.
3. Laura J. Corwin, 'Character and Morality in the Novels of Jane Austen', *Revue des Langues Vivants*, 38 (1972) 370, comments favourably on Brandon's understanding of decorum.
4. As a result critics refuse to believe in the change that has been wrought in Marianne. Mudrick, p. 93, argues that Jane Austen betrays Marianne. Tony Tanner, 'Introduction', *Sense and Sensibility* (Harmondsworth: Penguin, 1969) p. 32, claims that 'whatever the name of the automaton which submits to the plans of its relations and joins the social game, it is not the real Marianne'.
5. Morgan, 'Polite Lies: The Veiled Heroine of *Sense and Sensibility*', pp. 188–205. Although Susan Morgan's is the fullest discussion of this aspect of *Sense and Sensibility*, it was previously noted by Nardin, pp. 39–45, and Tanner, 'Introduction', p. 15.
6. There is little written on the formal social occasion in *Sense and Sensibility*, but Tanner, 'Introduction', pp. 20–1, offers some illuminating comments on the London ball.
7. The critics noted in note 4 both have considerable sympathy for Marianne, as has Duckworth, p. 105. However, for a masterly analysis of the insincerity inherent in Marianne's sensibility, see Tave, pp. 78–96.
8. A thorough analysis of the consequences of Marianne's tendency to limit herself to 'a society of two' is offered by Duckworth, p. 109.

3 PRIDE AND PREJUDICE

1. For a discussion of the significance of the arrival of 'four strangers' see Joseph M. Duffy, 'The Politics of Love: Marriage and the Good Society in *Pride and Prejudice*', *The University of Windsor Review*, 11 (1976) 6.

2. A number of critics would not agree with this statement, especially as it relates to Elizabeth Bennet. However, they do not discriminate between Elizabeth's relationships with the Meryton world and with Darcy. Among the best of these less sympathetic accounts of Elizabeth Bennet are Babb, pp. 118–24; Susah Morgan, 'Intelligence in *Pride and Prejudice*', *Modern Philology*, 73 (1975) 54–68; Tave, pp. 116–29.

3. The social basis of Elizabeth and Darcy's misunderstandings is discussed by Rubinstein, p. 124.

4. For a full discussion of the relationship between Art and Nature in *Pride and Prejudice* see Samuel Kliger, 'Jane Austen's *Pride and Prejudice* in the Eighteenth-Century Mode', *University of Toronto Quarterly*, 16 (1947) 357–70.

5. For an excellent discussion of perspectivism in *Pride and Prejudice*, see Duckworth, pp. 124–5.

6. Murray Krieger, 'Postscript: The Naïve Classic and the Merely Comic: *Pride and Prejudice*', in *The Classic Vision: The Retreat from Extremity in Modern Literature* (Baltimore: The Johns Hopkins Press, 1971) pp. 221–43, also sees a tight relationship between theme and form in *Pride and Prejudice*. However, he believes that 'trimness of structure' helps impose a false 'unity' on the society under examination (242–3).

4 MANSFIELD PARK

1. The part played by these houses has been discussed in detail by Ann Banfield, 'The Moral Landscape of *Mansfield Park*', *Nineteenth-Century Fiction*, 26 (1971) 1–24, and Duckworth, pp. 36–80.

2. This conflict of social values has been the subject of excellent studies by Butler, pp. 219–49; Tanner, 'Jane Austen and "The Quiet Thing"', pp. 136–61; and Fleishman, pp. 19–40.

3. I do not accept the argument that *Mansfield Park* condemns any form of wit or charm. Amongst those who take this position are Robert Alan Donovan, '*Mansfield Park* and Jane Austen's Moral Universe', in *The Shaping Vision: Imagination in the English Novel from Defoe to Dickens* (Ithaca, N.Y.: Cornell University Press, 1966) pp. 148–52, and Walter E. Anderson, 'The Plot of *Mansfield Park*', *Modern Philology*, 71 (1973) 26.

4. Fleishman, p. 61.

5. My thesis places great emphasis on the period of activity which separates Fanny's two periods of very different kinds of quietness. It thus runs counter to the argument put forward by Tanner, 'Jane Austen and "The Quiet Thing"', p. 137, that *Mansfield Park* is the story of a girl who triumphs by 'doing nothing'. Others who have emphasised Fanny's passivity are Lionel Trilling, '*Mansfield Park*', in *The Opposing Self* (London: Secker and Warburg, 1955) p. 212; Nardin, pp. 107–8; Gerry Brenner, '*Mansfield Park*: Reading for "Improvement"', *Studies in the Novel*, 7 (1975) 30. The fact that Fanny becomes active has been recognised by Butler, p. 236 and Alan Kennedy, 'Irony and Action in *Mansfield Park*', *English Studies in Canada*, 3 (1977) 164–75.

6. This triangle of forces is also discussed by Banfield, p. 14.

7. For a summary of the critical debate about the theatricals, see Fleishman, pp. 24–9, 89.

8. Joel C. Weinsheimer, '*Mansfield Park*: Three Problems', *Nineteenth-Century Fiction*, 29 (1974) 200–5, argues that Fanny exaggerates the virtues of Mansfield Park. However, it is clear that she is thinking more of the house and its traditions than of the actual behaviour of the Bertrams. For an excellent discussion of Mansfield Park *vis-à-vis* its inhabitants, see Rubinstein, pp. 134–9.
9. For an excellent discussion of the false liveliness of the Crawfords, see Tave, pp. 158–204.

5 EMMA

1. The interplay between ranks can be depicted more fully in *Emma* than in any of Jane Austen's other novels because, in terms of the social range it embraces, Highbury is the most complete of her communities. For discussions of this aspect of *Emma*, see Mary Lascelles, *Jane Austen and Her Art* (London: Oxford University Press, 1939) pp. 179–80, and Wendy Craik, *Jane Austen: The Six Novels* (London: Methuen, 1965) pp. 50, 134.
2. Hints that Highbury is in decline have been noted by G. Armour Craig, 'Jane Austen's *Emma*: The Truths and Disguises of Human Disclosure', in *In Defense of Reading*, pp. 235–55 and Lionel Trilling, '*Emma*', *Encounter*, 8 (1957) 49–59.
3. Mr Knightley in fact has far more land and a somewhat larger income than Mr Woodhouse (136). However, perhaps because of his age and because he has more to do with the other villagers on a daily basis, Mr Woodhouse is considered 'first in consequence' (7) in Highbury.
4. Jane Austen makes many references to distances and journeys in *Emma* while developing her theme of the need for increased mobility. The restrictions placed on Emma, for example, are underlined by the fact that she has never travelled even as far as Southend (101). Jane Austen is also concerned, however, to emphasise that mobility can quickly become restlessness. Frank Churchill, who flits all over England and several times expresses a longing to travel abroad (221, 365) is the prime offender in this area, closely followed by Mrs Elton's relatives, who dash back and forth between Bristol and London (306).
5. There has been little criticism of this aspect of Mr Knightley's character. However, the idea that he is infallible (see, for example, Edgar F. Shannon, Jr, '*Emma*: Character and Construction', *PMLA*, 71 (1956) 644–5) has frequently been challenged. See, for example, J. F. Burrows, *Jane Austen's 'Emma'* (Sydney: Sydney University Press, 1968) *passim*, but particularly pp. 9–13, and Charles A. Knight, 'Irony and Mr Knightley', *Studies in the Novel*, 2 (1970) 185–93.
6. Duckworth, p. 166, points out that predictability is the mark of the gentleman.
7. Susan J. Morgan, 'Emma Woodhouse and the Charms of the Imagination', *Studies in the Novel*, 7 (1975) 33–48, also comments on Emma's tendency to avert boredom by means of her 'imaginist's' manipulation of others. However, she does not note the limitations Emma imposes on her sphere of irresponsible behaviour. The same is true of other studies of Emma's development, with the result that most trace a rather simplistic movement from early irresponsibility to final maturity. See, for example, Joseph M. Duffy Jr, '*Emma*: The Awakening from Innocence', *ELH*, 21 (1954) 39–53; Shannon, pp. 637–46; R.

E. Hughes, 'The Education of Emma Woodhouse', *Nineteenth-Century Fiction*, 16 (1961) 69–74. Nardin, pp. 121–2, notes the selectivity of Emma's irresponsible behaviour, but fails to unearth the principles underlying her apparent inconsistency.

For arguments similar to my own about the role played by Emma's imagination in diverting her from responsible social involvement, see Patricia Meyer Spacks, *The Female Imagination* (London: George Allen and Unwin, 1976), pp. 125–6 and Tave, pp. 205–13.

8. There are, of course, other structural principles at work in *Emma*. Shannon, pp. 646–50, for example, mentions the role played by formal social occasions, but places his main stress on the three proposal scenes. J. S. Lawry, ' "Decided and Open": Structure in *Emma*', *Nineteenth-Century Fiction*, 24 (1969) 1–15, argues that 'superimposed upon the general pattern of fancy is the stronger and more natural pattern of rational marriage' (2). Joseph Wiesenfarth, '*Emma*: Point Counterpoint', in Halperin, pp. 207–20, suggests that the novel is structured according to the principles of the fugue.

9. Had her view of Robert Martin not been distorted by looking at him through the lens of her romantic conception of Harriet, Emma would have realised that he is very much a part of Highbury society. Although she is not personally acquainted with him, he is Mr Knightley's tenant, lives close to Donwell (360) which is only a mile outside Highbury, and does business in the village (29). Therefore, Robert Martin ought to be included within that tiny circle of people towards whom she acknowledges obligations, rather than dismissed as a member of the bourgeois world in which the only things of importance are 'profit and loss' (33).

10. Many critics have noted similarities between Emma and Mrs Elton. See, for example, Mudrick, p. 194; Duckworth, pp. 157–8.

11. For a good discussion of stasis and movement in *Emma*, see Joel C. Weinsheimer, 'In Praise of Mr Woodhouse: Duty and Desire in *Emma*', *Ariel*, 6 (1975) 81–95.

6 PERSUASION

1. Duffy, 'Structure and Idea in Jane Austen's *Persuasion*', p. 277.

2. In her next, and incomplete, work, *Sanditon*, Jane Austen seems much more ready to accept that in reality an acquisitive middle-class ethic is replacing the old gentlemanly ideal. Thorough studies of this aspect of *Sanditon* have been produced by W. R. Martin, 'The Subject of Jane Austen's *Sanditon*', *English Studies in Africa*, 10 (1967), 87–93 and B. C. Southam, *Jane Austen's Literary Manuscripts*, pp. 100–35.

3. A number of critics have recognised that *Persuasion* is a study of social change. These include Nina Auerbach, ' "Oh Brave New World": Evolution and Revolution in *Persuasion*', *ELH*, 39 (1972) 112–28; Duckworth, pp. 180–208; Duffy, 'Structure and Idea in Jane Austen's *Persuasion*', pp. 272–89; Rubinstein, pp. 172–90; Joseph Wiesenfarth, '*Persuasion*: History and Myth', *Wordsworth Circle*, 2 (1971) 160–8; John Wiltshire, 'A Romantic *Persuasion*?', *The Critical Review*, 14 (1971) 3–16; Thomas P. Wolfe, 'The Achievement of *Persuasion*', *Studies in English Literature*, 11 (1971) 687–700.

4. For a detailed study of the part played by luck in *Persuasion*, see Paul N. Zietlow, 'Luck and Fortuitous Circumstance in *Persuasion*: Two Interpretations', *ELH*, 32 (1965) 179–95.
5. For a reading of *Persuasion* which puts considerable emphasis on Anne's problems in being noticed, see Tave, pp. 256–87.
6. For a similar definition of the role of the confidante, see Margaret Drabble, *The Needle's Eye* (Harmondsworth: Penguin, 1973) p. 344. As a child Rose Vassilou becomes the recipient of complaints from her parents and the servants because she is 'a tenant of both worlds, belonging to neither' (344).
7. This ability to make temporary accommodation into a home is shared by other naval characters. See, for example, Admiral Croft's description of how he has managed to be 'snug' (170) at Kellynch, Deal, Yarmouth and Bath.

Index